INSPIRATIONAL MISSIONARY STORIES

INSPIRATIONAL MISSIONARY STORIES

Compiled by
Leon R. Hartshorn

Published by
Deseret Book Company
Salt Lake City, Utah
1976

Contents

VI

VIII

"He was a prophet just like Moses"

Richard O. Clark

*I*n the early part of December 1960, the streets of Solingen, Germany, resounded with the hustle and bustle of Christmas. Bright-colored packages with red and green ribbons were tucked under arms or carried in traditional net shopping bags. Ironically, the anticipation that filled the air seemed to leave few people in the mood to listen to two missionaries present the message of Jesus Christ and the restoration. Our spirits were, nonetheless, high as we walked from door to door, for the Lord had blessed us with abundant success.

As we knocked on the door of an attic apartment, the scuffle of feet was heard from within. There was no response to our appeal, so we knocked louder. There was no reply. Finally my persistent companion picked up a broom from nearby and beat on the door very loudly. This time the high-pitched voice of an elderly woman was heard crying, "I'm coming, I'm coming. Wait a minute!" As the door opened, a small figure with long braided hair smiled and invited us in. She apologized for her delay, stating that her hearing aid was not in good working order. She motioned for us to be seated on the worn green couch, whereupon she immediately commenced chattering about a variety of subjects. Our presence seemed to arouse little curiosity in her.

We listened patiently for several minutes, forming negative opinions about her receptiveness. There appeared to be little evidence that she could bring forth the interest and concentration necessary to understand the gospel.

After our feet were sufficiently warm, I interrupted her steady flow of words and asked to be heard for only a moment. We presented a condensed version of the restoration of the Church through Joseph Smith, bore solemn testimony to his divine call, and gave her the pamphlet relating his own story. We closed with prayer, asking that she read the pamphlet and promising that if she asked in faith, she would know that our message was true.

1

A few days passed before we returned. Our thoughts during the interim hadn't really focused upon this woman, for in our minds there was little reason for much hope. At the appointed hour we approached her apartment and were welcomed in out of the cold. There was remarkable silence in the room. Where confused speech had been our experience before, humble attentiveness now pervaded the atmosphere.

We began with a prayer. Then I inquired, somewhat testingly, "Have you read the pamphlet about Joseph Smith?" "Ja," she responded. "Have you prayed about it?" "Ja," was the reply again. "Do you believe that he was a prophet?" came the next question. "*Ja wohl,*" she replied, "he was a prophet just like Moses." The witness of the Spirit was unmistakably clear. It miraculously enlightened her intellect and attuned her spirit to the message we carried. There was no more chattering, no incoherence, only an eagerness to absorb more truth. Everything we taught from that moment on was received in the humility of a meek child.

The missionary lessons were presented in rapid succession. When the principle of tithing was introduced and the question asked as to her willingness to obey this commandment, she replied, "If it is necessary, I will sell my furniture to pay my tithing if this is what God wants." My eyes scanned the room, and in my mind I quickly concluded that the total value of all I saw could not have been much more than a hundred dollars. What faith! It was all she had, and she was willing to part with it without a second thought.

After each lesson was presented, we would sit back on the couch and drink hot milk and eat vanilla cookies. She told us of her children, ten of them, who had all been killed in the war. Her husband had also met death in action. She described how for twenty years she had met on the street corner each Sunday with the Salvation Army, singing and worshiping as they understood it. She wondered if it would be permissible to stop by to see these friends on the way to church and bid them all farewell.

Her baptism date was only a couple of weeks after we met her, two or three days before Christmas. As we knocked on her door that memorable evening, there she stood in her long black coat, her purse over her arm, anxiously awaiting this important event. Across her face was a white bandage, and a few bruises could be seen. We inquired concerning them, and she responded, "I was in town this afternoon and was struck by a truck. It knocked me down and I fell into a mud puddle, but never mind that. The devil is not going to keep me out of the Church. We're off!" she said as she closed the door behind her. The small branch was full of joy that evening as this true convert made a vow with the Lord.

A few days passed and it was Christmas Eve. Members of the branch were invited to the home of Brother and Sister Piotrowski for an evening of sharing the Yuletide spirit. My companion and I accompanied Sister Severin to the festivity. One cannot forget the joy as arm in arm we helped her over the frozen, icy path to our destination. This experience reflected the essence of what Christmas was all about. It taught the unmistakable lesson that the joy we bring to others returns to our own lives in rich measure.

"That book is the word of God" *Lloyd N. Andersen*

*W*e were on a typical small-town Canadian street that ran on for a half-mile or so and ended up in a plowed field. My companion had already drawn his pencil through the house number of the only house on the street where we had not made contact in the seven times we had tracted that portion of Stratford, Ontario. As we thought of the next to last house far down on the left side of the street and looked at the series of "NH's" (Not Home) by the address in our tracting book, it hardly seemed worth the time or effort to walk down there for one more try before we closed out that tracting district. Elder Johnson flipped the book shut and we turned away, expecting that it would be years before this section of town would be contacted by missionaries again.

I had not taken many steps when I stopped and said, "Elder, my conscience won't let me go on until we have tried that house one more time." So, for the sake of my conscience, we trudged down the street and knocked on the door. My companion had already started down the steps toward the sidewalk when, to my final knock, the door opened a crack and two eyes peered out at me, magnified greatly by thick-lensed glasses. Behind the glasses, a small, elderly gentleman became apparent, and we were graciously invited to sit with him around a magnificent carved table that all but filled the living room of the tiny house. The little man warmly "brothered" us instantly, so from the moment we met him, he became Brother Davis to us. We introduced him to the Book of Mormon and gave him a copy, which he promised to read.

Before leaving the house, I offered a prayer, in the middle of which Brother Davis bellowed out, "Amen!" I was taken aback and supposed that I may have spoken so softly that the old man thought I was through. Speaking louder, I resumed the prayer only to be stopped again by another resounding "Amen!" Wondering if I had prayed long enough that our host was indicating he felt I ought to quit, I

4

brought the prayer sincerely to a close. We learned later that Brother Davis had belonged to a religious group where it was customary to voice agreement to various things that were said in a prayer by saying "Amen" frequently during the prayer. When we suggested that we thought we could show agreement with one "Amen" at the end of the prayer, he thought that made sense and never again interrupted as we prayed with him, although his "Amens" at the end seemed to come forth with the extra force of the several that he restrained himself from giving in the middle.

A few days later, we made a return visit to check on Brother Davis's progress with the Book of Mormon. As we sat once more around his elegant table, a quick glance revealed the open Book of Mormon and a large magnifying glass resting beneath an extraordinarily bright table lamp, a laborious and difficult reading system necessitated by his obvious visual handicap. After exchanging a few pleasantries, I took a deep breath and said, "Well, Brother Davis, I see you've been reading the Book of Mormon. What do you think of it?" I have never forgotten either the manner or the content of his reply. Picking up the magnifying glass and shaking it toward us for emphasis, he said, "Boys, that book is the word of God!"

During the ensuing discussions, it became almost humorous for Brother Davis to remark, "Teach me something else. I already believe that." Elder Johnson and I decided to give him a discussion on baptism for the dead, which we were sure would be unusual enough to have escaped his avid study of the scriptures. To our astonishment and delight, when we began our presentation he indicated that he had pondered the fifteenth chapter of 1 Corinthians and had already come to the conclusion that baptism for the dead was a valid principle. All we were able to do for this good man was to acquaint him with the mechanics by which the principle was exercised in the temples of the Lord.

So ready for baptism was Brother Davis that we jokingly told him he had been a Mormon all his life and just didn't know it. He agreed with us and soon made it official in the waters of baptism.

5

Sometimes a cold shudder of memory sweeps me back to that street, and with a twinge, I recall how very close we came to walking away from one of the most golden of contacts a pair of missionaries ever found. That only lasts a moment or two. I am quickly warmed by a surge of gratitude for an active conscience and the sweet Spirit of inspiration that made this memorable experience possible.

The wrestling champion
of Niue Island

*T*he island of Niue Fekai is in the South Pacific near the center of Polynesia. At the time I served a mission there, it was headquarters of the Niue Island District of the Tongan Mission, and The Church of Jesus Christ of Latter-day Saints had been on the island less than six years. The natives are a beautiful people both in spirit and in simplicity.

One memorable day my missionary companion and I were returning from the back of the island when we chanced upon a large crowd on the large green near the center of the village of Alofi. From the perimeter of the crowd, I could see six big barefooted natives dressed in khaki shorts, preparing for a wrestling contest.

Suddenly I heard my name called. The pastor of the island's London Missionary Church was pointing at me over the heads of the crowd and beckoning me to enter the circle. It was then that a horrible suspicion entered my mind. The pastor explained to the natives in their own tongue (which by this time I was understanding only too well) that since the caucasians had not been represented in their contest, it was fitting that Eleta Tomosoni (Elder Thomson) should do the honors. Looking at those six men from within the circle, I thought I had stumbled onto a South Pacific branch of the Los Angeles Rams. When I heard the rules being read for the finals in the Niue Island Wrestling Championship, I thought I was finished! What was even more disconcerting was the fact that I had been teaching the boys in our branches of the Church to wrestle so they could compete as sportsmen, with good sportsmanship being stressed. In the crowd I saw some of the faces of those boys who had been in my wrestling sessions. Like a skunk turning upwind, I realized that I could not back out gracefully.

I finally agreed to wrestle one of the men—but was further disheartened to learn I would have to wrestle all six! Names were being drawn out of a hat to determine in which

7

order they were to be wrestled, not just which one would compete.

At that moment the full force of their size emerged. With my six-foot, 200-pound frame I had ranked in the upper percentile of the male population of the world, but now I observed that I was the same size as the smallest of the six Niuean village champions.

I glanced toward my companion. He was about 150 pounds and five-foot-seven or so. No support from that quarter. Placing my hands beneath my chin in a prayer-like fashion, I indicated to him that we needed all the help we could get. He responded by looking at his watch—I suppose to see how long it would take for the wrestlers to annihilate me.

I drew the first name, which belonged to one of the largest of my opponents. He stepped out of the group and squared off, as I quickly rehearsed the rules in my mind. Somehow I had to get him down with both of his shoulder blades touching the ground—that was all. I did not even have to hold him down while someone counted to three in Niuean or English.

The handkerchief was dropped, and he was running at me. From that point the facts slip into oblivion. I recall his coming at me, and I vaguely remember getting hold of him and using his own momentum to throw him off balance and to the ground. Afterward, try as I will, I cannot recall anything else that happened until well after the contest was over. Later my companion told me that he had been watching his watch, and when the referee dropped his handkerchief, the time started; when the opponent was downed, the clock was stopped. It had taken a cumulative total of 47 seconds for me to down that entire battery of native warriors, and I was the Niue Island Wrestling Champion!

There is no question in my mind what had happened. Before the contest, we had been harassed, rocks had been thrown at us, and we had been chased out of native villages with bush knives. But now there was a perceptible change. The natives would go out of their way to greet us with the

Niuean *fakaalofa*, or greeting. We were on the way to being accepted. Through the Spirit of the Lord, one missionary had been rescued, and the way had been opened for missionary work on Niue Island.

"I want you to knock all the cement off these steel posts," the boss said as he handed me the sledgehammer and stood back to watch me begin. Anxious to impress him with my eagerness for the task, I planted my feet in a wide stance, raised the sledgehammer high above my head, and brought it down hard on the barrel-sized keg of cement caked on the first leg of the extracted guardrail.

Six—seven—eight solid follow-up strokes to the same spot, but all I could feel was the stunning reverberation up the handle of the sledgehammer. Not a single chip of the hard cement seemed to yield under the blows. After resting the hammerhead on the ground for a moment and rubbing my right shoulder, I again raised the hammer high above my head and repeated the effort, but with no better result.

I felt a little embarrassed as the boss watched a minute longer. Then, starting to walk toward the tool shop, he said, "I'll get you something that may help."

As I had arrived for work that morning wearing ankle-high work shoes, with cowhide gloves dangling from the back pocket of my denims, I had wondered, as I had on the two previous mornings, if this would be my last day on the job. I hoped not. With only three months before I would enter the mission home, I needed every penny I could earn to help cover my mission expenses, at least for the first few months.

Dad said that no sacrifice by the family would be too great for the privilege of supporting me in the mission field, and he meant it. He knew what that kind of sacrifice was. I remember how the family had spread margarine on the bread and then scraped most of it off again while my older brother Ron was in the mission field. I also sensed Dad's special gratitude when occasionally I was able to spare a few dollars of the earnings from my part-time job to add to what was sent to Ron.

Yes, I knew it would mean sacrifice, gladly offered. I also knew I had to do all I could.

I took a firmer grasp on the handle, holding it a little lower this time to get a better weight advantage from the heavy steel head. Several more strokes, and now I could feel myself becoming angry. How could I strike any harder? Why didn't the cement break?

"I hope he doesn't get back before I've shown some kind of progress," I said to myself, glancing toward the tool shop.

When I had told the boss on Monday morning that I had quit school to work for a few months so I could go on a mission, I had hoped he would think kindly of me. Instead he had said, "Why do you want to waste your time like that?" Since then he had seemed bent on going out of his way to make snide comments about the Church and other crude remarks that I suspected were designed to shock me. But he was the boss and the one who would let me stay or let me go.

I had been much more comfortable the previous week when I first got the job and was helping Bert Godfrey lay a brick wall to replace an old wooden one that had burned down. How could I help but like that leather-faced but kind-hearted man who had served three missions, two of them building missions.

The company had hired me for ten days, mostly to help build that wall. But Bert and I had worked so well together, we had finished it in a week. He didn't seem to mind that I was a bit clumsy and lacked experience. He knew I was trying and he knew why. He just kept talking to me about serving the Lord.

Bert hadn't told me that the real boss was on vacation, and it had come as a surprise when I showed up for work the next Monday morning. So far, though, my strategy seemed to be working. Although I was earning more than I had ever earned before, I figured that if I worked so hard that I was worth still more than they were paying me, maybe the boss would feel he just couldn't afford to let me go.

I looked again at the long I-beam rail with thirteen legs extending from it like a giant comb with most of its teeth missing. It had long ago served as a bumper guard, preventing cars in the parking lot from hitting the adjacent building. It had been installed by digging thirteen large holes in the ground in a straight line, spaced at eight-foot intervals. A steel post was cemented into each hole, and the connecting bumper rail welded to each post. Recently the entire rail had been removed by having two large cranes extract the whole thing in one piece, and it was lying in the driveway with each post encased in a barrel-sized cement block.

As I heard boots scuff the loose gravel on the asphalt pavement leading from the tool shop, I let loose a wild flurry of blows. I was glad that a few beads of sweat had formed on my forehead. "Here, try this," the boss said, as he handed me a heavier sledgehammer. That wasn't quite the kind of help I had in mind.

I smiled as I handed him the smaller hammer, but I could tell that he sensed it wasn't a completely honest smile. He watched me for a few minutes more and then, without further comment, turned away to supervise the crew working on the remodeling project in the steel fabrication plant.

"The only difference between the hammers is that this one is heavier and harder to lift," I grumbled to myself, as the steel head collided with the stone-hard cement. Finally one small chunk broke off. After several more strokes my arms started to ache, but the cement still remained intact.

At this rate I knew it would take me three days to complete the job. I also knew that if I didn't show substantial progress by noon, I'd be out of a job and back standing in the labor lines at the Employment Security Office taking any kind of work available. Three days of that had made me especially anxious to keep this job.

Besides, it was 1954, and thousands of striking workers with families to feed were looking for short-term, full-time employment. How was a twenty-year-old boy going to compete with them for the few jobs available?

It took only a few more hard but unsuccessful strokes to

persuade me that I had reached my limit and it was time for me to treat the problem as one needing more strength and wisdom than I possessed.

Resting the heavy hammer on the ground and trying to compose my anger and frustration, I felt the need and desire to discuss the problem with the Lord. Without either kneeling or closing my eyes, I started praying aloud to the Lord and explaining the task I faced. In a conversational but sincere way I reminded him that I wasn't asking for the money so I could buy a yellow convertible. He had called me on a mission, and I knew he wanted me to go. This job had already been the answer to my prayers, but I needed to keep it. I didn't expect him to send a host of angels from heaven with sledgehammers, but I knew he could help me.

Never in my life has a prayer been answered more immediately or clearly. Suddenly my mind was filled with a thought so lucid and strong that my heart started pounding. It was a simple solution, as I later considered it. To brighter or more experienced minds it might have occurred earlier, but to me it came as a direct answer to my prayer.

The compelling instruction said to me, "Instead of striking the cement, strike the steel."

Still not fathoming exactly why, I raised the hammer and brought it crashing down five or six times on the steel post right next to the cement. As a large section of the cement cracked into big chunks and fell off, I realized that the blows to the steel had started a series of strong vibrations that were transmitted all along the steel shaft.

I quickly forgot the weight of the hammer. With new energy I struck the steel again and again, then moved on to the next post, amazed at the magnification of my efforts as the steel vibrated and the cement cracked.

Less than two hours later I had removed the cement from all thirteen posts and had stacked the large chunks in a pile. With the sledgehammer on my shoulder and a prayer of gratitude in my heart, I went to find the boss.

"I'll need some help moving the railing out of the driveway," I said, trying to conceal the excitement I felt inside. Thinking I was giving up on the project, he motioned me to follow him to the parking lot.

As we rounded the corner of the building and he saw the railing and the pile of cement, he stopped quite suddenly. His eyes blinked and opened wide. His chin started to drop a bit. For a full minute he stood silently, looking first at the railing, then at the cement. After a moment more he turned, motioned me to follow him again, and said, "Come on, I'll give you another job."

Nothing more was said about the incident, but the following morning when I arrived for work, he simply said, "Lloyd, you're welcome to stay on as long as you like."

I worked there for nearly three months before entering the mission home. He then let me come back to work again for another ten days until I departed with my group for the mission field. Never after that memorable morning did he, in my presence, make a disparaging remark about the Church or my plans to serve a mission.

Many times since that day the Lord has helped me strike the steel instead of the cement in solving other problems. But as I departed for the mission field in late November 1954, I knew that I was called of the Lord. I knew that he was listening to my prayers. And I knew for myself that he would give no commandment save he would prepare a way for it to be accomplished.

New Era, October 1975, p. 26. Used by permission of the author.

"You a number one Christian"

George Durrant

*W*orld War II, combined with other world events, in an indirect way opened the door for increased interest in Christianity in South Korea. During the period following the Korean War, I was there as a member of the United States Army.

Shortly after arriving in this land, I observed that some people were excited about Christ and his teachings, but at the same time, the Koreans were confused because the good they had read and heard about Christianity was quite different from the questionable conduct observed in soldiers who supposedly were Christians.

Korean civilians came into our camp each day to perform the menial tasks that were undesirable to us, such as K.P. They, in turn, were paid, and the arrangements made both groups happy. As they went about our camp they, like us, used the dirt paths that led between the weeds and other growth. When American soldiers and Koreans met on the paths, the Koreans jumped aside into the weeds while the soldiers proudly passed by.

As I observed this situation, it occurred to me that this was not the way things should be. This was their land, and we, if anyone, should move off the paths. Therefore, I made it a practice to move aside and let the Koreans pass on the path. They seemed amazed but also pleased. Soon I learned many of their names, and as they passed I greeted them by name.

Months passed and I learned some of the ways that the GI's had created to communicate with the Koreans. One rather unusual system consisted of a way to describe the goodness or badness of something by calling that which was very good "number one" and that which was very bad "number ten." For example, if we were talking to a Korean about our good jeep, we would say, "This is a 'number one' jeep." Or if it were a wreck, we would say, "This is a 'number ten' jeep."

15

It was a rule at our camp that if a soldier held the rank of corporal or higher, he would enter the mess hall and go to a table where a Korean worker would bring him his meal. All who had lesser rank went through the line for their own food.

One day I entered the hall, noticed the line was long, and sat down at a table with five of my friends who were eating while I waited for the line to get shorter. As I talked to the others at the table, I felt someone at my elbow. I looked up, and standing at my side with a tray of food was one of the Korean workers. I realized that he was about to put the tray before me, so I pointed to the stripe on my arm and said, "You can't serve me. I'm just a private."

He looked down at me with moistened eyes and quietly said, "I serve you. You a 'number one' Christian!"

I know why the Korean worker judged me so. It was because of the little things I'd done. It's the little things that make a "number one" Christian, and the little things that, when added together, make up a big thing called life.

Improvement Era, November 1968, p. 82. Used by permission of the author.

I should like to begin my story by relating a little of my background. I was born in Sioux City, Iowa, and reared thirty miles south of there in a small community called Whiting. Our family—my parents, a brother, a sister, and I—attended sporadically the Congregational Church. As I look back, I believe I attended mainly for social reasons, and although I said my prayers each night, I don't believe I ever thought deeply about the existence of God.

One day in 1962, when I was in high school, I was walking home with some of my friends when something caught my eye in the window of a local store. I paused to look closer while my friends continued to walk slowly ahead, except for one who lingered behind and was closer to me. I slowly turned to continue walking with my friends when suddenly I felt myself being pulled with great strength out of the way of a car hurtling in the air toward me. The driver's foot had evidently slipped when he tried to brake and he had hit the gas pedal instead—and the car had jumped the curb and headed directly at me. My girl friend had somehow sensed the danger I was in and turned in time to pull me to safety. The car crashed into the store where I had been just seconds before, causing considerable damage to both the store and the car.

As I walked home that day I pondered in my heart the great power of God, for now I knew he existed. I began to consider my relationship with him and realized that had my life been taken, I would have died without ever having completed the first step given for me to return to him—to repent and be baptized in the name of Jesus Christ for the remission of my sins.

In my church a confirmation class was being held for youths my age to prepare them for baptism and confirmation. I had never enjoyed the classes before, but now I approached the minister and asked him to direct me in completing whatever was necessary so I might join the group in confirmation and baptism. He was angry with me and asked why I hadn't attended the classes regularly. Frightened but determined, I explained that I just hadn't been ready for them. He could see that I was determined, so he reluctantly agreed to outline a program for me. Once he saw that I was true to my word, he allowed me to join the group, and I was baptized by sprinkling and confirmed a member of the Congregational Church.

When I was a senior in high school, my family moved to Denver, where I met a young woman who introduced me to her church—called an interdenominational church, though they favored Baptist-evangelist teachings. At one of the first meetings I attended, the minister asked, at the end of his sermon, for anyone wishing to give his life to Christ to come forward and stand before the altar. My friend and I went forward. We were escorted to a little room where we were questioned as to whether we were ready to accept Christ as our Savior. I said that I felt I had already accepted him, but now I understood that accepting Christ as my Savior meant something different to them than it meant to me, and I was quite interested. So I became active in this new church.

I was invited to attend some lectures given by the minister on the beliefs and doctrines of other churches. One evening he spoke on the Mormon Church. I remember laughing with everyone else at the lack of credibility in the Mormon beliefs. Who could believe that an angel would appear to a man on the earth in this day and age, and with the strange name of Moroni? The doctrine of baptism for the dead was totally incomprehensible to me, and the belief in a book of scripture as important as the Bible was sacrilegious. Being totally ignorant of the true doctrines of the Mormon Church, I had no reason to doubt the minister. And so, for many years I too went around with false assumptions about the Mormons—they were a strange people.

My second encounter with the Mormons came as I went with a group from my church to do some tracting at the airport just outside Denver. I had never tracted before, so I wasn't sure what was expected of me. The group was reluctant to ask me along because of my inexperience, but one of my friends reassured them that I would do fine. I was handed a sheet of paper and told to talk with the first person I met and ask that person for a few minutes of his time for a survey of churches. The questions all led up to one big question: "Have you accepted Christ as your Savior, and will you give your life to him right now?"

I was petrified, but a friend headed me down a concourse and followed behind me. Taking a deep breath, I approached a soldier sitting alone and asked to talk with him for a few minutes. He seemed pleased and treated me with respect and courtesy. I was very surprised at his knowledge of the Bible, so I finally asked him what religion he professed. "I believe you would know it better by the name of Mormon," he said.

In our conversation he told me that he believed in Christ and had accepted him as his Savior. I was more than satisfied; I hadn't really "saved" him, as I had been told to do, but I sincerely felt that he was already saved. Never did he try to disillusion me in my beliefs; he showed extreme patience. I found out that he was returning from Vietnam with a bullet wound in the head. There was not a bit of bitterness in him; rather, there was a gentleness.

This was the last tracting group I was ever asked to join, perhaps because I told my friends that I felt the young man was already saved.

One day a young man asked me to accompany him to a revival meeting. I accepted because I was curious; I had heard that unusual things sometimes happen at revivals and that God is present. I will never forget the cold feeling I had when I walked into the assembly hall. I was appalled by what the people were calling the spirit of Christ. I could not find it within myself to accept the fact that he would require his followers to degrade themselves in worshiping him. The God I loved was a God of love and order, not a God of confusion and melodrama. Though I loved the people there and knew many of them personally, I could not honestly feel

19

that the Spirit was leading them. On the way home I told my friend how I felt, and he replied that Satan was probably after me. He said that he would try to rebuke him, so he placed his hands on my shoulders and began speaking in what he called "tongues." I was frightened, because that was not how I had pictured direct communication with the Lord to be.

Even though I felt this way, I couldn't let go of this church because I knew of nothing better. Then a young man I had dated steadily for over a year was killed in an automobile accident. He was not a member of any church, but was a very good person. For comfort I automatically went to my church, where a well-intentioned young seminary student told me that my friend could not be saved because he had not said, "I accept Christ as my Savior." He told me I would be far better off if I accepted that fact as quickly as possible and worked harder for the living. For over four months I could not get out of my mind the thought that my friend would be forever damned just because he had not actually said the words "I accept Christ as my Savior." Even though in my heart I knew better, I feared it might be true. Soon I stopped going to church.

I still earnestly felt the need for God in my life, and I never stopped praying to ask him to show me that he was a personal God and that those who died without a knowledge of him or who did not fully understand his gospel were not condemned to hell, but were loved by him. I received my answer one Sunday night when two friends and I stopped to eat at a drive-in restaurant. Soon a car drove up behind us, and a group of squealing young men and women ran excitedly to my car. I recognized them as a group from the interdenominational church. They began to tell me that they had been having a prayer circle and my name suddenly came to them. They felt inspired to go immediately to find me to tell me that God loved me and cared about what I was doing. They were amazed that they had found me so quickly in a city of more than a million people. The friends I was with thought the group was fanatical, but my heart was calm, for now I knew that God was exactly as I thought him to be—a God who cared for each individual. He had not forgotten me. I felt no need to return to that church, because in answering my prayers God had told me, through these young people, that he cared for me as a person, and thus he cared for every other individual on the earth, and all were not lost. I did not understand how the dead would have their opportunity, but it was enough to know that they did, and I could stop mourning now.

In 1966 I met my husband-to-be, John W. Max, and one year later we were married. He was a staunch Catholic, and I agreed to attend his church with him, thinking that perhaps its doctrines would help me find God. I was willing to learn, and for over three years I went with John to his church, but we never discussed religion. He was a good Christian, and though we did not discuss religion in depth, we did have regular family prayer, and this strengthened our marriage.

In 1970 we moved to Alexandria, Virginia, and I accepted a position at a private Catholic girls school. It was there that I had my third encounter with the Mormon Church.

I attended a staff dinner where I sat beside a young girl who was very friendly. Somehow we began talking about religion. She told me that she was a Mormon convert and proceeded to briefly outline her religion to me. I said that it was by far the most beautiful religion I had ever heard about, but it was so beautiful that it was like a fairy tale, and I wondered how people could believe in fairy tales. I rationalized that it couldn't possibly be true, since everything was so perfect—and also since I had heard so many derogatory things about the church. Then I quickly forgot about it.

One day I was reading a magazine article about a famous minister whose son had committed suicide because of drugs. The minister felt that somehow his son was trying to communicate with him, and so he contacted a clairvoyant and came to believe that he had indeed made contact with his son. Because of some of the things the son supposedly said to him via the clairvoyant, the minister came to some crushing conclusions: that Jesus was not the Christ, since the spirit world where the son dwelt was separate from heaven and hell; and since the spirits were not released to go to God, Jesus was not the link after all.

I could not and would not draw the same conclusions about Christ. Was there actually a place where the dead went to hear the gospel and to be given every opportunity before meeting God? Who had the answers?

At school I was approached by one or two nuns in regard to Catholicism. I welcomed this, and at the suggestion of one nun, I agreed to go to a priest and ask to take lessons so I could have a fuller understanding of the Catholic doctrines. I approached not only one priest, but three; but for various reasons I was turned away by each.

By this time I was very discouraged. I had been to church after church looking for something (I knew not what), and I felt that I was at the end of my rope. I *had* to know if there was a true church or not, and I had to know it with every fiber of my body. My only solace now was in prayer. I picked up my Bible, read a few verses, and then knelt beside my bed. With tears streaming down my face, I poured out my heart and soul to Heavenly Father. I cried out, "Oh, God, please help me. I am so very tired of looking. I have been everywhere. If one of these is your church, then why do you keep shutting the door in my face? I just don't know which way to turn. Do you even have a true church on the earth? I need to find you. I'll go wherever you lead, but please guide me. If you show me the way you want me to go, I promise I will go, no matter what the cost." I continued praying for some time, and when I finally arose, I felt at peace. I knew that sometime, someday, God would answer my prayer. I just needed to wait on him.

John wouldn't be home until later that evening, and I had work to do before he came, so I got my wash together and took the elevator down to the main floor of our apartment building. I had forgotten something, so I returned to our floor. As I stepped off the elevator and began to walk toward my apartment, I saw two young men standing at my door. My heart began to burn and I trembled, because I knew that they were from a church and had been sent in answer to my prayer—and I knew that Heavenly Father wanted me to know this. As I approached them, it was with rejoicing in my heart, but fear also.

One of the young men smiled and said, "Do you live here?" I replied that I did, and he said, "We're from The Church of Jesus Christ of Latter-day Saints. Would you like to hear a little about our church?"

At that time I did not know that this was the formal name of what I had heard called the Mormon Church. I thought that perhaps this was some little church no one had ever heard of before. I invited them in, and as we talked, I found out that they were Mormons, and my old prejudices came back. But I decided to be open-minded and to listen so I could give their message a fair chance. After all, God had sent them, so there must be two sides to what I had heard.

They discussed the Church briefly and asked if they could come back and meet with my husband and me and explain their beliefs in greater detail. I told them my husband was a strict Catholic and I wasn't sure he would listen, but I would ask him. As they left I shut the door and leaned against the wall, saying incredulously, "The Mormons, Lord? The Mormons! *They* are *your* people?" Then, with thanksgiving in my heart, I entered my bedroom, knelt by my bed, and thanked God for answering my prayer. I also asked him to please soften John's heart so that he too would believe.

When John came home and I told him I had met some nice young men from the Mormon Church and that they wanted to come back and tell us about it, he said that if that was what I wanted, fine, but he was not about to change religions. I told him I didn't expect him to, but I did want him to listen to the missionaries with me. I didn't dare tell him what had happened, at least not yet. Finally he smiled and said, "If it will please you, I'll listen." My heart was overflowing. He had never before even been willing to discuss his religion with me, let alone any other religion, and now without a doubt God had softened his heart.

The elders called back and we scheduled an appointment. When they came, they offered a beautiful prayer and gave us the first discussion. We didn't ask many questions, probably because we didn't really know what to ask. We agreed to another appointment, and after they left, John said, "I really enjoyed that." They had left us a copy of the Book of Mormon to read. Just having that book in the house affected me. Normally I am a rather heavy sleeper, but while the book was in the house, I would wake up in the middle of the night with an overpowering urge to read it. I had no doubts about its being true, because the Holy Spirit continually bore witness to me.

As the elders continued the lessons, new and beautiful concepts were unfolded to us. For the first time we could understand the Bible. Then came a real challenge—the Word of Wisdom. John had a closetful of liquor, and I was a chain smoker. I had tried many times to quit smoking, but just couldn't do it. Now I had to quit. I was frightened to think that a cigarette could stand between God and me. Then a scripture came to my mind: "Ye cannot serve God and mammon." (Matthew 6:24.) Both John and I made our decision for God that day.

Although we were doing everything the missionaries asked us to do, John's background still nudged at him, and he insisted that we also attend the Catholic Church. We attended Sunday School at The Church of Jesus Christ of Latter-day Saints on Sunday morning and mass at the Catholic Church in the evening.

It was hard for John to imagine how early Book of Mormon prophets crossed the ocean from Jerusalem to the Americas. He had been in the navy for four years, and it seemed unbelievable to him that the Nephites could cross the ocean on flimsy boats. He prayed about this and the following day an article appeared in the Washington *Post* telling about Thor Heyerdahl's expeditions in papyrus reed boats.

That morning after Sunday School one of the missionaries asked us if we were coming to sacrament meeting, and John said, "Oh, no, we have to go to mass." I didn't say a word because this was John's decision and not one I could make for him.

Mass and sacrament meeting were both at four o'clock, and at about 3:40, John put down the paper he was reading and left the room. A few minutes later I wondered what he was doing, so I went to the bedroom. Through the doorway I saw him kneeling in prayer beside the bed. I turned quietly and walked back into the living room. When John came out, he went to the closet, got my coat, and said, "Come on, dear, we're going to sacrament meeting. We've gone to the Catholic Church for the last time."

On July 18, 1970, John and I were baptized and confirmed members of the Church by our wonderful missionaries, Elders Dennis Christensen and John Brent Hall. We are so grateful for their prayers, for their many hours of service to us both before and after our baptism, for their strong testimonies of the gospel, and for their love for us. We are also grateful to their families for their sacrifice and support so they could serve the Lord and help us find our way back to God.

We believe that we have the most wonderful families in the world, and we love each one of them dearly. We pray that someday they too will understand and realize the importance of finding the truth, which can be found only through prayer, study, and a desire to serve the Lord. This has been only the beginning for us. We have much more to learn, but we know that God does live, that he sent his Son to earth, that through Christ's atonement we might return to our Heavenly Father, and that he has unmeasurable blessings for each of us. We pray that we might be able to pass our love of the gospel on to our children, and they to theirs, so that we may find happiness together.

"He leadeth me"
to my conversion

Gwen Boyer

I grew up in a nonreligious home, though my parents did send me to Sunday School at the local Methodist Church in a suburb of Adelaide, the Australian city called "the city of churches." For some strange reason, even as a child I felt a strong desire to be a missionary, not knowing why or how such a thing could be accomplished.

Increasing conflict at home led to my father's leaving us and going to Queensland. I was only fifteen years old, but I also decided to leave home; I had to discover life for myself.

Fifteen is not an ideal age for experience to calm the tempestuous sea of life. Instead, my foolishness caused me great pain as I drifted from place to place and job to job, all over this large sun-drenched continent. I met and mixed with many undesirable characters, seeking thrills and excitement but always feeling empty and unwanted, longing for that elusive peace of mind that never came within reach. Many Christian people I knew were evidently happy, but their disciplined way of life could not be lived by me—or so I thought. How I admired them! How I wished I could be like them, but how futile for me to try!

Finally, after drifting aimlessly from city to city, always ashamed of my past, always hoping that each new place would mean a fresh start, a new life, I arrived in Darwin, the northernmost city of Australia. Darwin is somewhat isolated from the major centers of population and thus provides a haven for many who want to forget the bright lights and hustle and bustle of the big cities. It also provides an opportunity to hide from the world and lose oneself among many who seem to be going nowhere and trying to get there fast. Thus my life pattern became drink, drugs, and anything else that promised erasure of reality. And for once in my life I became frightened. I felt that I was losing my faculties, and I even questioned my sanity. Though this might be considered "rock bottom," it was also a great turning point in my life.

One night as my fevered brain wandered, my thoughts struck upon the teachings of my childhood. I recalled someone preaching about a loving Savior and a kind Father in heaven. I felt a strong urge to pray, but how, and to whom? If Jesus was the Savior, I thought, he might teach me to pray.

I knelt at my bedside and awkwardly uttered some meaningless words. Oh, how I wanted to do it right! "Help me, help me," I pleaded silently. Tears came easily, and deep shame and sorrow filled my heart. It was then that I felt a warm assurance come over me. I sensed that a message was trying to get through to me but somehow could not. Then a painful realization struck me. I had to make peace with my father and obtain his forgiveness first before greater help could be given. This was my test.

That night I wrote to my father in Queensland, begging his forgiveness and acceptance once again. My driving objective now was to get home to Adelaide, where my brothers and mother lived. I had to change my way of life and work toward having a more united home. Soon after, I heard from my father—sweet words of love and forgiveness. I had moved home to the welcome of a loving family. I knew how the prodigal son felt, and I was glad.

Now the work of building a new life began. The Bible had the answers, I thought, and so I read and reread that great volume of scripture, searching in it for the answers to a happy life. I searched among the many churches for the way, the truth, and the life, but always I came away gloomy and dissatisfied. My constant prayers were becoming more meaningful yet frustrating.

I felt a great need to be baptized, but how, and into which church? One day my ardent desire led me to approach a local priest about baptism, but seeing the state I was in, he refused, telling me I had to wait until the regular baptismal service some months later. Concerned and feeling rejected, I was beginning to despair again; however, a glimmer of hope led me to believe that I must be patient and endure further trials before I would find the true church.

27

Over a period of two months, while traveling to and from work in the city, I noticed some young men with displays in a public square teaching about a restored religion. My curiosity was aroused, and I wanted to investigate their teachings, but I didn't know what to do about it. I felt fearful of being coerced by their teaching.

Then one day a knock came at our door. Two young men stood there and asked if I knew that there was a prophet living today, indicating that the Lord had not forgotten his people in this age. Something made me feel good about this statement. My mind raced as I connected these two men with those whom I had seen in the public square, and I felt I had to know more. I didn't have time to hear their message that day, but I purchased a copy of the Book of Mormon from them and promised that I would read it.

My first impressions of the book were lukewarm, but the testimony of Joseph Smith seemed to strike me as a significant occurrence in these troubled times. It could be true, I thought, and I determined to build on my experience of faith and prayer to ask the Lord if it was a true account.

Illness and pressing events deferred further investigation at that time. During my convalescence, however, I had a nagging feeling that I should read the Book of Mormon. I read parts of it, being in a hurry to know what the book was generally about. As I read it, tears came to my eyes. I knew that the stories in it were true and were of God. I had to know more, and so I called the nearest branch of the Church. A friendly voice seemed excited to answer my request for more information about the church and promised to send the missionaries to my home.

Ten long days later, the missionaries visited me. My impatience had caused some anxiety over what I had done, but looking back now, I know there was one more test I had to pass before I was fully prepared to be taught by them. A week after I had called the church, I was overcome with a tense feeling. I had turned to drink and cigarettes for solace in the past, but this time I could only feel disgust at myself for turning to these evils for relief. Prayer had to be the answer, so all that night I was in and out of bed and on my knees struggling for some kind of comfort from the Lord. Once again he accepted my prayers, for I felt assured that all would be well and that he would take care of me. From that day, the Word of Wisdom was a principle to which I was truly converted.

The missionaries came on Sunday, and Elder Doyle's first words bore testimony that the Church was true and that his testimony was given in the name of Jesus Christ. These have to be men of God, I thought. To me they were perfect. I began taking the discussions with them.

Three days of fasting and prayer, which I did independent of any request by the missionaries, seemed unnecessary, since I knew all along that the message of the gospel was true. I wanted to be baptized after the first discussion, but the elders restrained my enthusiasm and asked that I pray for assurance. I was sure, and so the following Friday, just under one week after I was first taught by them, I was baptized and confirmed a member of The Church of Jesus Christ of Latter-day Saints.

Part of the blessing I was given was that I would become a missionary. What a confirmation of my childhood desire to serve the Lord in this very way! As a member of the true church, I have found that my perspective of life has changed radically. I am pursuing another childhood desire to practice nursing and hope one day to be able to serve a full-time mission.

In many ways I feel I have come home. The Holy Ghost is a real and comforting personage. Prayers are answered when they are sincerely offered. I am so happy and grateful for having found the gospel, and I pray that others who have had similar experiences will also find the encouragement of the Spirit that I did and also make it home.

A real
Latter-day Saint

Yu, Kum Ok

I am a housewife with one son and two daughters. I am thirty-four. I was married in 1964. I would like to express my testimony.

I was baptized on September 14, 1974, and I am proud of my husband, who is a real Latter-day Saint in Korea. Even though he was baptized just four years ago, I think he is such a great person; he made up his mind to be a Jesus-like man. After he was converted, I didn't know anything about the meaning of life. I had questions, such as, Where did we come from? Why are we here? Where are we supposed to go? I thought that there was no God, and that Jesus was a mere normal person. All I had in mind was to help my husband and keep my children strong and growing. I never cared about salvation, that is to say, everlasting life.

But now I am quite different. I know the meaning life really has. Through the deeds and words of my husband, I have come to know what Mormonism really is. My husband never drinks, smokes, no coffee, no tea, and he comes home right after he finishes his work. He never takes offense, and he likes to play with the children, wash the dishes, keep the house clean, never tells a lie, always tries to speak soft words and do house chores as willingly as he can. All these things, I see through my own eyes. I think there is no other miracle like this. My husband was converted into quite another person.

After my husband was converted, I wondered what made him so different a person. Finally I understood. It was the Book of Mormon, which he always read. I made a decision to enroll in an institute class to learn about the Book of Mormon, and I studied with American missionaries whom my husband introduced to me. At last I was baptized by my beloved husband. I think, this same power-spirit that made my husband quite another person now influences and blesses me also.

Now I want to live for time and eternity with my hus-

band and children in the home of celestial glory. I would like
to be a devoted Relief Society member, good mother, and
good wife who sustains always in the doings of the
priesthood holder, my husband.

A fire truck fills the font

Kirk Magleby

*I*n November 1973, Elder Craig Lark had only recently been made senior companion. He and his Peruvian companion, Elder Gonzales, were working in the pleasant little town of Taena in the southern Peruvian desert, near the Chilean border. They had been teaching the Lopez family for several weeks, and the following Friday was to be their baptismal service. Brother and Sister Lopez had been excellent investigators, and the elders were excited to see them coming into the Church.

On Friday the elders hurried to the little chapel to make arrangements for the baptism. While Elder Lark began preparing the white clothing, Elder Gonzales put the plug in the font and turned on the faucet. To his dismay, no water came out.

The missionaries hurriedly checked the faucets in the restrooms and kitchen and discovered that there was no water in the building. In fact, they checked around the neighborhood, and all water was off—and no one had any idea when it would be available.

Elder Gonzales knew that water shortages are commonplace in his native country, especially in the arid parts along the coast. Elder Lark, anxious to see the Lopez family baptized as planned, sat down and began to suggest alternative ways to get the font filled. Taena is an oasis in the desert, and water is a precious commodity. There were no public swimming pools, no large rivers nearby, and the ocean was almost thirty miles away. Besides, Brother and Sister Lopez had their hearts set on being baptized by a member of the branch presidency in the lovely font in the chapel they had come to love.

Then Elder Lark thought of asking the fire department for assistance. Elder Gonzales chuckled at the idea, but people would be arriving for the baptism in less than two hours, and the elders were getting desperate. They hurried to the fire station at the other side of town. The lieutenant on duty scoffed at their request. "What would happen," he asked, "if a fire broke out while my men had the pumper truck at the Mormon chapel?" Though the elders persisted, he didn't relent. "Impossible!" he exclaimed, with an air of finality in his voice.

Undaunted, Elder Lark took occasion to ask the lieutenant the golden questions, to which he replied that his parents had been Catholic, he was Catholic, and he would always be Catholic. However, he was just enough impressed by the elders' persistence that he smiled as they started to leave his office, and he suggested that they try the water department.

The man in charge of the water department, after hearing their request for one of his tank trucks to fill up the font for a baptism, was incredulous. "Why so much water, if all you do is this?"—and he made a little sprinkling motion in the air with his fingers. "No, no," Elder Lark replied, and he opened his flipchart to the picture of the Savior being baptized by John the Baptist in the River Jordan. Then he turned to the picture of a modern baptism and told the surprised chief of the water department, "This is a baptism in the true church, and we do it by immersion. Now, may we borrow one of your tank trucks, since the water is off in our chapel?" The chief muttered something about the lateness of the hour, but he allowed Elder Lark to use his telephone to call the fire department one more time.

This time Elder Lark decided to contact the fire captain. With less than an hour left before the baptism, this would be his last hope. He reached the fire captain at home and explained his problem. The captain agreed, and he called his lieutenant while Elder Lark and Elder Gonzales hurried back to the fire station. The lieutenant himself was on the big pumper truck, waiting for them. Siren blaring, he drove through the main street of town with the two elders on the seat beside him.

They arrived at the chapel just five minutes before the service was to begin, and the firemen hooked a hose to a hydrant across the street, amid cheers of church members who had gathered to witness the baptism. The firemen ran the hose through a basement window and into the font, filling it up in minutes, then drove away as members of the little branch continued cheering.

It was a deeply spiritual service that day, one that drew the members of the Taena Branch closer together than they had ever been before. Brother and Sister Lopez have since moved to Chimbote, farther north in Peru, and he is the seminary coordinator for the Trujillo District of the Peru Lima Mission.

"That will depend entirely upon you"
Orson F. Whitney

*P*rior to leaving home, I had done little writing and less speaking, neither hoping nor caring for success along either line. But now I was seized with a strong desire to write, especially to describe scenes beheld and incidents noted during my travels. Forthwith I began a correspondence with the *Salt Lake Herald*—first, however, writing to the editor, Byron Groo, and asking him if that paper would publish what I might send. He promptly replied, "thanking me in advance" and encouraging me to proceed.

My communications to the *Herald*, the first one dated March 14, 1877, leaped at once into popular favor. This gratified me, of course, but I became so absorbed in the correspondence that it encroached upon hours that should have been given to religious study. Elder Musser chided me for it. "You ought to be studying the books of the Church," said he. "You were sent out to preach the gospel, not to write for the newspapers." I knew he was right, but I still kept on, fascinated by the discovery that I could wield a pen and preferring that to any other pursuit except the drama, my ambition for which had been laid aside.

Then came a marvelous manifestation, an admonition from a higher Source, one impossible to ignore. It was a dream, or a vision in a dream, as I lay upon my bed in the little town of Columbia, Lancaster County, Pennsylvania. I seemed to be in the Garden of Gethsemane, a witness of the Savior's agony. I saw him as plainly as ever I have seen anyone. Standing behind a tree in the foreground, I beheld Jesus, with Peter, James, and John, as they came through a little wicket gate at my right. Leaving the three apostles there, after telling them to kneel and pray, the Son of God passed over to the other side, where he also knelt and prayed. It was the same prayer with which all Bible readers are familiar: "O my Father, if it be possible, let this cup pass from me; nevertheless not as I will, but as thou wilt."

As he prayed the tears streamed down his face, which

was toward me. I was so moved at the sight that I also wept, out of pure sympathy. My whole heart went out to him; I loved him with all my soul and longed to be with him as I longed for nothing else.

Presently he arose and walked to where those apostles were kneeling—fast asleep! He shook them gently, awoke them, and in a tone of tender reproach, untinctured by the least show of anger or impatience, asked them plaintively if they could not watch with him one hour. There he was, with the awful weight of the world's sin upon his shoulders, with the pangs of every man, woman, and child shooting through his sensitive soul—and they could not watch with him one poor hour!

Returning to his place, he offered up the same prayer as before; then went back and again found them sleeping. Again he awoke them, readmonished them, and once more returned and prayed. Three times this occurred, until I was perfectly familiar with his appearance—face, form, and movements. He was of noble stature and majestic mien—not at all the weak, effeminate being that some painters have portrayed, but the very God that he was and is, as meek and humble as a little child.

All at once the circumstance seemed to change, the scene remaining just the same. Instead of before, it was after the crucifixion, and the Savior and the three apostles now stood together in a group at my left. They were about to depart and ascend into heaven. I could endure it no longer. I ran from behind the tree, fell at his feet, clasped him around the knees, and begged him to take me with him.

I shall never forget the kind and gentle manner in which he stooped, raised me up, and embraced me. It was so vivid, so real. I felt the very warmth of his body, as he held me in his arms and said in tenderest tones, "No, my son; these have finished their work; they can go with me; but you must stay and finish yours." Still I clung to him. Gazing up into his face—for he was taller than I—I besought him fervently: "Well, promise me that I will come to you at the last." Smiling sweetly, he said, "That will depend entirely upon yourself." I awoke with a sob in my throat, and it was morning.

"That's from God," said Elder Musser, when I related to him what I had seen and heard. "I do not need to be told that," was my reply. I saw the moral clearly. I had never thought of being an apostle nor of holding any other office in the Church, and it did not occur to me even then. Yet I knew that those sleeping apostles meant me. I was asleep at my post—as any man is who, having been divinely appointed to do one thing, does another.

But from that hour all was changed. I was never the same man again. I did not give up writing, for President Young, having noticed some of my contributions to the home papers, advised me to cultivate what he called my "gift for writing." "So that you can use it," said he, "for the establishment of truth and righteousness." I therefore continued to write, but not to the neglect of the Lord's work. I held that first and foremost; all else was secondary.

Orson F. Whitney, *Through Memory's Halls*, pp. 81-83.

"If I only had
two years to live"

Since returning from the mission field, I have been contemplating the principles of the gospel that have influenced my life, and I think I see one principle above the rest. It is given in the scriptures:

"There is a law, irrevocably decreed in heaven before the foundations of this world, upon which all blessings are predicated—

"And when we obtain any blessing from God, it is by obedience to that law upon which it is predicated." (D&C 130:20-21.)

I would like to tell you how I discovered the truth of this principle.

When I went into the mission field as a new elder, I was sent into a small, northeastern industrial city. The people were mostly of the same traditional religion; and though they made up a melting pot of nationalities, they seemed indifferent to new ideas. A large percentage of them were older people; even the buildings seemed old.

My companion, Elder Kenneth House, whom I learned to love dearly, had been serving there before I arrived, with very meager response. And after we had worked together for nearly two months, we were still meeting with little success. We had contacted about three-forths of the city, but we had given very few discussions. Discouraged, we decided the thing to do was to reevaluate our program and determine what was wrong.

At this time we were studying the Doctrine and Covenants. We had read the passage in Section 130 that promises that if we will live the laws on which blessings are predicated, we will receive those blessings as a matter of right, because our Father in heaven will be bound. (See also D&C 82:10.) We determined to outline the laws that governed success in the mission field and to commit ourselves to them with all our hearts:

a. We would live both the spirit and the letter of the

law where mission rules were concerned—get up on time, have early morning study classes, be in on time, etc.

b. We would bear strong, sincere testimony at every door and to every contact.

c. We would exercise the power of the priesthood and the power of the fast.

d. We would study and pray—thus opening the channel of revelation that concerned our city, listening to the Spirit's direction.

e. We would take advantage of the minutes.

Then we went to our Heavenly Father in prayer, asking him for strength and guidance in our efforts. We began to fast. I believe this was on a Thursday. We fasted for two days, and at the end of the second day we had not received the blessings we were seeking. Yet we felt that during that time we had humbled ourselves and adhered to the laws in every way. In order to find contacts we had gone the extra mile many times, working without rest breaks and continuing from door to door each evening long after we were tired and wanted to quit. That Saturday night we were so discouraged we felt like going home and just sitting down to lose ourselves in self-pity. We almost felt that the Lord had ignored the laws we were trying to live. We broke our fast.

That evening we went out seeking appointments, still with little success. In discouragement, we finally went to the home of a member of the Church who was working on the "every-member-a-missionary" program. When we arrived, the family wasn't home, but the grandmother was there. Since she was not well, we stopped to talk with her for a few minutes. When the phone rang, she asked me to answer it. On the other end of the line was a lady who wanted to know if the people of this particular home were members of the Church. I replied, "They are."

"Well," she said, "a month or so ago two young men dropped by my home and left a Book of Mormon with me. They have not been back to pick it up, but I know the book is true and I would like to learn more about the Doctrine and

Covenants and the Pearl of Great Price that I read about in the footnotes."

The two young men who had "dropped by" that home were Elder House and myself. We had not followed through on the contact. We had slipped. We had not written it down. But in answer to our prayer and in answer to directly living the laws of fasting, humility, and perseverance, we were blessed with the response of this woman.

She was baptized, and later so was her husband. It seemed the Lord had tested us right to the last minute and then blessed us beyond our expectations with a contact who was baptized only a few weeks later. The city seemed to blossom from then on, and as long as we lived the "law of success" we were blessed with the response of the people.

After I left this particular area, I received a real challenge. With a new companion who had been in the mission field even a shorter time than I, I was called to open a city in upper Michigan that had never before been "worked" by missionaries. Before we got there, we knew only that there were two adult members of the Church and four children. We were anticipating the challenges waiting for us. Our first responsibility was to get a home Sunday School started so these people could attend each week. We held a home Sunday School the first week we were there, and all six members in the city attended. At that time I recalled that the Church was started in the same way in 1830, with six people. I hoped this was a good omen.

From previous experience, we had anticipated the great missionary challenge of this city. We went through the city exactly as Elder House and I had gone through the one where I was first sent, and again we did not have any success. So we sat down and reevaluated our program and decided we must rededicate ourselves to our work. And it was following this rededication that I was blessed with the most rewarding spiritual experience of my life.

We had decided we must do what Oliver Cowdery and David Whitmer did as they anticipated their missionary work. Early in the morning we climbed to the top of the hill that overlooked the city (they called it a mountain, but it was very different from the mountains we had known at home in Utah) and there we knelt down and used the priesthood to dedicate the homes, the people, the very soil of that city, to our Father in heaven. As we knelt, the sure witness came into my heart that we were engaged in the work of the Lord and that we were going to find success in this place. Getting up from my knees, I looked at my companion, Elder Gordon Smith, and the tears were rolling down our cheeks as we witnessed the Spirit of our Father in heaven.

We went forth again in that city. Two days later we knocked on a door, and a lady answered. When we told her who we were, she said, "I am not interested, but my husband may be. Would you like to come back at night sometime?"

That was all there was to it. But when the woman closed the door, I turned to my companion and said, "These people are going to be members of the Church." One of the gifts a missionary is given is the power of discernment. Three weeks later the husband and wife were baptized.

I mentioned the elder I worked with in my first city— Elder Kenneth House, a wonderful young man. He was truly one of the most dedicated elders in the Great Lakes Mission and was loved alike by older members of the Church and the new contacts he baptized. He had a magnetic personality, and because of this he was a leader in the mission.

Elder House was like a brother to me. Unless you have been on a mission, you cannot understand the deep relationship you can have with a companion. This love existed between us, and we stayed close, even after we were no longer companions.

One afternoon I received a phone call from President Berg, the mission president.

"Elder Affleck," he said, "Elder House had been in an automobile accident. We are going to fast for him in the mission. I would like you to call on the elders in your zone and ask them to fast."

I made the phone calls. Then I went to my room and closed the door, and kneeling down at my bed, I poured my heart out to my Father in heaven. I begged him to bless this young man whom I loved so dearly, that he might live. About three hours later, President Berg called again and said, "Elder Affleck, this man you loved so dearly has passed away."

I remember hanging up the phone and pounding my fists and saying, "Why? Why Elder House? He was serving his Father in heaven. Why did he have to be taken at this time?"

And I received the sweetest feeling. I knew Elder House was still serving his Heavenly Father. He had been transferred to do missionary work on the other side of the veil.

I realized that my desire that my friend should live was not the will of my Father in heaven. Soon afterwards I was asked to do the hardest thing I have ever done. I was asked to write a letter that would be read at Elder House's funeral. As I wrote this letter, I recalled something he had once said that impressed me greatly. We were at a group meeting. There, a young man our age declared that he could not figure out why two young men in the prime of their lives— the years supposed to be the most fruitful and productive from an educational and social viewpoint—would give up so much to do missionary work. Elder House looked the man squarely in the eye and said, "If I realized that I had only two years to live, I would live them serving my Father in heaven!"

Instructor, June 1969, p. 200. Used by permission of the author.

Baptized in
a therapy tank

Shane Rowley

*W*hile laboring in Gainesville, Florida, I met Joel Norris. One Sunday at church a lady walked up to us and asked us to visit her nonmember husband, who was in the Veterans Hospital. She explained that he was being examined for malignant tumors. She told us he wouldn't be interested in the Church—he belonged to another church—but we were welcome to visit him and see what we could do.

We visited Joel that day and just talked with him and listened to his life story. He was very friendly and invited us back. From then on we visited him every other day. It seemed that every time we went to visit him, a member of his church would be there to try to start an argument. We never contended with them. Later, Joel said this was the first thing that softened his heart toward us and the Church. He said that he could tell we spoke with authority and in honesty, and that we wouldn't contend.

Not long after we met Joel, he received some bad news. The doctors found malignant tumors in his head, his spinal column, his lung, and his leg. They said he wouldn't live another year. By this time we were very close to Joel, and it was a big shock to us all. I have never seen a man as afraid as Joel was at this time.

The doctors finally decided to operate and remove the tumors in his head and spinal column. The operation would require moving a bone from his lower leg to his back to support the vertebrae when the tumor was removed. The doctors were very skeptical.

The night before his operation, Joel asked to be administered to. We gave him a blessing and promised him he would completely recover. I could just feel the Spirit bearing witness to me that Joel would recover. He was still scared, but he said that he felt a surge of peace from that time on.

Somehow Joel survived the operation. Then he spent weeks in intensive care struggling with death, but the Lord

43

preserved his life. When he was finally discharged from the intensive care unit, he was placed on a Stryker frame and not allowed to move, even an inch, or his spine would collapse.

We continued to teach him, and we could feel the Spirit very strongly with every discussion. Joel started testifying to friends in his church that he knew our message and the priesthood power were real. We challenged him; he cried and thanked us for coming into his life with the gospel. It was very rewarding.

Joel's faith was so strong that he wanted to be baptized as soon as possible. At the risk of his life, he was baptized in a therapy tank on the Stryker frame. If he had slipped at all, he might have died or, at least, have been paralyzed for life.

Today, Joel Norris is an active member of the Lord's church and is almost completely healed. The doctors are amazed.

*I*t was probably raining when I first met Charles Malcolm Webb, Jr. In Japan it was usually raining in March.

But rain or no rain, our meeting had a great impact on my life, and no one knows how many others.

One evening, late in March 1957, I was walking casually from my barracks to the snack bar on Yokota Air Base near Tokyo, Japan.

I was deep in whatever thoughts occupy the mind of a lonely eighteen-year-old boy thousands of miles from home when a voice jolted me to reality.

"Dave, wait up a minute."

Turning in mid-step, surprised to hear my name called, I saw Charles trotting toward me in the night.

As he approached he asked, "Going to the snack bar?" I said I was, and he asked if he could accompany me.

"Sure, I'll buy you a cup of coffee," I offered, wondering who he was. Everyone in the squadron knew me—I was the squadron mail clerk, but I knew very few of my fellow airmen, except by the mail they received.

"No, thanks," he said. "I don't drink coffee."

"How about a cup of tea?" I asked.

"I don't drink tea either," he replied. "I'm a Mormon." He paused, then added, "What do you know about the Mormons?"

It was to be several years before the General Authorities were to ask members of the Church to ask their friends the golden questions, but his question was no less effective.

Charles and I had walked less than a block together when he asked me, "What do you know about the Mormons?" I had yet to learn the name of the young boy I was talking with but I took the bait—hook, line, and fishing pole.

By the time we arrived at the snack bar, I had discovered with whom I was talking. Charles was a few months

45

younger than I, a convert to The Church of Jesus Christ of Latter-day Saints, and he held the office of a deacon.

For nearly three hours, he told me about the Mormons and their beliefs. I didn't understand half the things he told me, and probably listened only because he was enthusiastic about his religion.

Seeming to exhaust his knowledge of the gospel, he invited me to accompany him to the home of his branch president, Frank Moscon, an officer living off base with his family.

We walked the few blocks to Frank's home together, and somehow Charles found more things to say about his church.

Charles knocked on the door. When it was opened, I met the man who was to take me into the waters of baptism.

We were invited in, and Charles told Frank that I would like to know more about the Church. Before we returned to our barracks, a cottage meeting had been set for the following evening.

There was no end to Charles's enthusiasm. On our way back to the barracks, he invited me to attend church with him on the following Sunday.

On June 1, 1957, I was baptized by Frank at Camp Drake, a U.S. Army camp a few miles from Yokota Air Base. I would have been baptized a few months earlier, but being a minor, I had to write home for my parents' permission to join the Church. After it came, I had to wait several weeks for the next scheduled baptismal.

When Charles and I left Japan, we were both priests. I didn't hear much from him for a long time. Then I learned that he was serving in the West Central States Mission. The news hardly came as a surprise to me. He will be released from his mission this summer, and I am looking forward to meeting him again for the first time since we left Japan.

A lot of wonderful things have happened to me since I met Charles. In May 1962, I married a lovely LDS girl, in the Salt Lake Temple, and a few weeks ago, our first child was born.

Whenever I count my blessings, and "name them one by one," I always start with the day I met Charles Malcolm Webb, Jr.

Improvement Era, July 1963, p. 591. Used by permission of the author.

Truth, light, conviction

Lucile McNeil

*N*earing my fifty-fourth birthday, and with eighteen months behind me in The Church of Jesus Christ of Latter-day Saints, "I stand all amazed" as I recall the succession of events leading to my rebirth in the waters of baptism.

One evening two young Mormon missionaries called at my home and announced their ministry. I let them know, most emphatically, what I thought of the Mormon Church. They didn't say another word, but turned around and left. I have thought often of that episode since I've been in the Church, and I've speculated what the course of my life might have been had I come into the Church at that time.

Years passed. I began to be vaguely troubled about the mystery of life. I did not worry what would become of me after death; oblivion was the answer to that, I was sure. It was ridiculous to think of people living with a God. But the idea of being alive at all had me wondering, and I became introspective. I thought of an insect, alive one moment, then stepped on and dead the next. Whence had fled that bit of animation? What was the source of it? What was the source of it in me—in all life?

I considered the starry heavens and the planets whirling in space, never colliding, but each always in its own orbit. When I was about fourteen years old I had seen Halley's Comet, and if I lived to be ninety years old I would see it again. There was order in the universe—a marvelous precision. And I was certain that man had nothing to do with it. But who? Where? What?

Maybe the religionists had answers after all, but I felt it was no use turning to them; I had already examined their teachings, and nothing in any of them appealed to me as having truth, conviction, or light. I would concede that there was an Almighty Being, or what you might wish to call God, but one man's guess was as good as another's as to his nature, and *never* could I believe in a personal God who heard and answered prayers and who saw each sparrow as it fell.

48

Then I went to jail, sentenced to spend five days for contempt of court. I anticipated a lot of time for reading. However, library privileges were available only once a week, and I was too late. There was nothing to read but some Catholic Bibles, tracts, and pamphlets, and they held no interest for me. I devoted my time to writing instead. The morning I was to be released I was ready half an hour early. I could not abide idle waiting, so I took down a Catholic booklet from the shelf and began reading. For the first time in my life I began to see that Jesus was of divine origin.

When I returned home, I didn't know quite what to do with my new knowledge. It was but a spark of the basic creed of religionists, and it seemed I could go no further. Deep personal conflicts were troubling me, and I forgot about Jesus.

I was in this state of despair when, for the second time, I was visited by Mormon missionaries. This time I was a little more approachable than I had been the first time. I assured them I knew all about the Mormons, so they left me a copy of the Book of Mormon.

The book gathered dust for about a year, and then two more missionaries came along. To my surprise, they knew about the Book of Mormon left with me and asked if I had read it. Of course I had not, and what was more, I didn't want to be bothered about it. No one could possibly explain God to me!

Over the next few weeks I got to know the missionaries—Elders Evan Stevenson and Spencer Palmer—better. Wherever we met—on the street, in the post office, in my office—they were always polite and friendly and interested in me. They were so friendly, I just couldn't get angry at their persistence in always wanting to talk about the gospel.

Then one day they had some news for me. They were without purse or scrip! I thought it was scandalous for a church to expect its missionaries to live that way—always at the mercy of others for room and board. Well, at least I could help out. I had a guest room, and I told them they were welcome to stay there as often as they liked and also to share potluck with us. I was dismayed when they said they could accept these accommodations only if they were allowed to preach the gospel to me in return. Well, all right, but that didn't mean I had to listen (though I didn't tell them that).

On a blistering hot August afternoon in 1948 the missionaries came to stay at my home for the first time. Because of the heat I brought them tall glasses of iced tea—which they refused. I learned a little about the Word of Wisdom then, and I substituted milk for tea.

Since I am over 50 percent deaf in one ear, the elders had to raise their voices. We were sitting outside, and I was afraid the whole neighborhood was going to hear about the gospel, they had to speak so loud. At the end of the discussion I decided that if I had to listen, I would do it in the house after that.

The elders came about once a week, and I let their message go in one ear and out the other. My constant taunting comment: "Do you really believe *that?*"

One evening, after a particularly fruitless discussion, Elder Palmer told me that they would not be back. They had not come out on their missions to make casual friends, but converts to the restored gospel of Jesus Christ. I was sorry, but we parted friends, with a warm handshake.

Then Elder Stevenson was transferred, and one day I saw Elder Palmer with a new companion. As always, he had a hearty handshake; and when he introduced his new companion, Elder Reed Bowen, I saw that he too was warm and congenial. I asked them to come see me. Elder Palmer hesitated but finally agreed to come for supper and to spend the evening.

After supper they washed the dishes (which Mormon missionaries always insisted on doing) and then we settled down for a gospel discussion. Elder Palmer opened his scriptures to the first section of the Doctrine and Covenants. I had heard this scripture before, but this time was different. Suddenly excited, I asked him what else he could tell me that was as reasonable and believable. He turned to Ecclesiastes,

Job, and Proverbs and discussed preexistence. Now here was something I could grasp. This made the gospel come true. Why had I never heard about this in other churches? Elder Palmer explained that The Church of Jesus Christ of Latter-day Saints was the only Christian church that taught this doctrine of preexistence. A feeling welled up in my breast that I had never experienced before. I *knew* that Jesus was of divine origin! Elder Palmer afterwards told me that the Holy Ghost had been responsible for my seeing the light after so long.

I was baptized February 19, 1949, by Elder Palmer, and Elder Bowen confirmed me afterwards. From that hour I have felt nothing but steady spiritual growth in the Church. There can be no possible question that Joseph Smith was a prophet of God; no possible question of the divine origin of the revelations he received; no possible question of the Book of Mormon being the word of God; no possible question of the priesthood power in these days being solely in The Church of Jesus Christ of Latter-day Saints.

I humbly thank my Heavenly Father that I was allowed to hear the gospel again after having rejected it; that I was blessed with meeting and learning from such missionaries as Elders Stevenson, Brown, and Palmer—men whose righteous lives are an example to the Church and to the community at large, and whose devotion to the gospel stands out as an inspiration to the weak in faith. I thank my Heavenly Father for the many blessings that have come to me in the Church, and I pray that his Spirit will guide me always.

A German girl's prayer answered

Heidi Bahlinger
as told to Edwin O. Haroldsen

In the spring of 1969, Heidi Bahlinger was teaching religion at a junior college in Freiberg, Germany. She was meeting several classes of sixteen- to twenty-year-old youths twice a week to discuss their own and other religious beliefs. They were sometimes joined by the Catholic priest of the college.

Heidi had been teaching for seven years and had shown such talent that she had been promised a year off at full salary to work for her master's degree.

One afternoon she and her mother were shopping when they saw a street display by some Mormon elders. Heidi talked with the elders a while and finally asked them to come to her classes to talk about Mormonism. They accepted the invitation and introduced their faith by showing the film Man's Search for Happiness. *Afterwards they answered questions. One hour for each class was not enough, so they came back on other days to continue the discussion.*

Heidi relates what happened then and in the weeks that followed:

The Catholic priest responded to the missionaries' teachings by pleading for his own religion. I tried to present the Lutheran theology. During these first hours of discussion, I defended my beliefs by quoting Bible verses that showed the truth as far as I knew it. The missionaries, too, proved their truth with the Bible. When I realized that their answers made much sense to me and could just as well be as true as mine, I stopped defending and started to listen. I can truly say I became interested in what the missionaries had to say. One day, after a discussion, I found myself saying, "I really would like to know everything about your faith." It surprised me that I said this. It almost sounded to me as if somebody else had said these words. Yet I felt very honest and sincere about this request.

After having seen the movie a few times, I began to like

52

it. My initial resistance gave way. At first it sounded too fantastic, too unreal to me. The world as I knew it had little to do with the philosophy this movie carried. Nephi's words " . . . and men are, that they might have joy" (2 Nephi 2:25), spoken and illustrated in the movie, were so different from what I called reality. The question then came to me: Is this a reason why it cannot be true, or could it be true in spite of what I have encountered?

Another thing that prompted me to listen more carefully to the teachings was the personal witness of the two missionaries. I could not explain what it was, but I sensed strongly a great authority in what they said, and even more so in what their personalities reflected. The first evening the missionaries came to my place to arrange for their visit to my classes, they spent some time talking about general things. I had a friend visiting with me that evening. When the missionaries had gone, I turned to my friend saying, "What was this? I felt something radiating from them both. They must have been praying." My friend agreed. This "something" that I had no other name for was also with them when they were teaching in my classes. It fascinated and puzzled me. Their knowledge of the Bible and their intelligent approach toward the students and the teachers contributed greatly to my trusting in them and their words.

I guess it would not have been too difficult for me to move on in a deeper understanding of what they taught had I not stumbled within myself each time when they mentioned the Book of Mormon and their "other books." I was certain that here they must be on the wrong track. To me there was only one book—the Bible. I started out to seek for more explanations by asking some of my friends, Protestant, of course, what they thought about the Book of Mormon. Their answers were negative.

Without being asked, my Catholic colleague came to warn me never to read the Book of Mormon. Finally, I found some literature on the Mormons. In Germany, there is no lack of anti-Mormon literature, but I must have picked the worst of all. It was very confusing to me to know that the author of the material was an accepted theologian. For days I wrestled with what I read. Needless to say, I found myself in great conflict. On the one hand was the witness and teachings of the missionaries; on the other hand, forty pages of shocking statements about the Mormon doctrines. It appeared to me that the only way out of this conflicting stage was to ask the missionaries not to come back to my classes anymore. Thus I hoped to be able to forget what had previously been said by them. However, I did not feel comfortable in choosing this rather cheap way out. Over and over I turned to God in my prayers, asking for guidance and light in my decision. Through these prayers, I gained courage and a definite feeling that I should face the missionaries again. As had been planned, they again came to my school. Again we spoke and decided on a date when they could come to speak with me alone.

When they came to visit with me, they brought me a gift. When I found out that it was the Book of Mormon, I was greatly disappointed. I told them that I would be very skeptical if I read the book. They left, and I did not feel a need to ask them to come back. Both the missionaries and I knew that any further discussion would entirely depend upon my response to the Book of Mormon.

It seemed strange, but I picked up the book right after they had gone. In my fear to read it, I knelt down and asked God to forgive me for wanting to read it. Then I opened the book, started reading, and kept reading through half the night. Why? Because my feelings changed completely. I relaxed. While I read I kept on praying: God, help me to understand what I am reading, and show me whether or not it is thy word, thy church. How fast that prayer was answered! The words started to light up. The testimony of Jesus Christ in the Book of Mormon started to burn within me. I knew it was the power of the Holy Spirit that surrounded me.

Within one week I had finished the reading of the Book of Mormon. Not only did I know it was true, but I also began to pray for courage to face the consequences this newfound treasure demanded.

How much I needed courage for the following days and weeks! It was a very dramatic way of losing almost everything that had seemed important in my life up to this time. My concept of God, of Jesus Christ, and of the Holy Spirit was changing. Many questions concerning the understanding of myself began taking on a new meaning. A reflection of my former life and beliefs had to be faced. Oh, how far reaching a conversion can be!

I had to stand up and bear testimony to my parents, my relatives, my friends. I also had to give up my job and all the planning I had made for my near future. These were not easy things to do. They were so much against my nature. It surely was no fun to have the people closest to me turning against me. The pain felt by many about my decision was very real.

Some important questions needed to be answered. What was I going to do to find a new job? How would I gain more insight and deeper understanding in the teaching of the gospel as I knew it then? The pressure of the German society, which I had already experienced, indicated that it would be difficult to find a job equal to what I had done and what I loved to do. Germany had no seminaries where I could study the Book of Mormon, LDS theology, and church history. Therefore, it was a relief and new hope to me when President Orville Gunther of the South German Mission suggested that I go to BYU, that I use my saved money to gain a new education and a stronger understanding of the LDS faith.

I am aware that conversion, baptism, and receiving the gift of the Holy Ghost are just the beginning in my journey as a member of The Church of Jesus Christ of Latter-day Saints, but I have taken a very decisive step.

Since her conversion Heidi has been graduated from Brigham Young University and is currently teaching in a military language school in California. Active in her ward,

Heidi serves as a stake missionary and as the representative for the Special Interests group.

New Era, April 1975, p. 11. Used by permission of the author.

Kresimir Cosic— basketball and baptism

Dick Davis and Duane Hiatt

"**Y**ou can tell a Mormon," people say. "He stands out in a crowd."

This one does. He ascends 6 feet, 11 inches, standing in his size 17 shoes. Yet with this towering frame he jumps like a gazelle. He has more moves than Bobby Fischer and more tricks than Harry Houdini. He's an Olympic star, an all-American honorable mention, a European all-star, and the highest scorer and rebounder in the history of Brigham Young University—the Yugoslavian giant, Kresimir Cosic.

A native of Zadar, Yugoslavia, Kresimir has led his hometown team to the Yugoslavian national championship and represented his nation at the Mexico City and Munich Olympic Games. The team won a silver medal at Mexico City in 1968.

He has traveled all around the world playing basketball for Yugoslavian and European all-star teams.

From 1969 to 1973 Kresimir established himself as one of the best, if most unorthodox, centers ever to play in the Western Athletic Conference, leading BYU to two conference championships in three years.

He was a nonconformist from the start, doing such uncenterlike things as leading the fast break on the dribble, potting long outside shots, going in for two-handed, underhand lay-ups with his knees tucked under his chin, and shooting underhand shots along the baseline against towering defenders. Perhaps his passing was the most spectacular element of the game; he hit men he didn't even seem to be looking at and who didn't even seem to be open. Flying up and down the court, his long limbs moving in ways unknown to medical science, the man from Zadar earned such nicknames as "the wild giraffe," "the runaway camel," and "the tallest guard in the league."

In November 1971 Kresimir was baptized a member of the Church. He lives his religion with the same determination and gusto with which he plays basketball. Kresimir's teammates at BYU report that after his conversion he could seldom be seen without a Church book in his hands—on planes and buses, in hotel rooms, or wherever he was.

Since leaving BYU, Kresimir has returned to Zadar, where he works as the general manager of Zadar's basketball teams, selecting and training the coaches and also playing on the number one team himself. In Yugoslavia, amateur athletic teams are sponsored by cities and clubs instead of by schools. Kresimir also plays for Yugoslavia in international competition. In the recent European championships, which Yugoslavia won, he was voted a member of the all-Europe team. Part of the championship Yugoslavian team, led by Kresimir, visited the United States and won six out of eight games against Big Eight competition.

The drastic change that has taken place in Kresimir's life-style since he joined the Church has prompted questions from many of his thousands of fans, and he answers them with the confidence that comes from hard study and real conviction. Answering these queries is often a real challenge, because most members of the younger generation in Yugoslavia have no background in any type of religious belief, lacking even the religious vocabulary common in such discussions.

Kresimir's devotion to his religion prompted *Tempo,* a prominent sports magazine, to conclude sadly, "Kresimir's stay in the USA has made him a religious fanatic." His travels with the Yugoslavian national team have given Kresimir the opportunity of visiting many branches and wards of the Church in many different lands, and he never misses a chance to visit with the Saints.

Kresimir is practically idolized in his hometown of Zadar, and he returns the feeling of warmth. An Italian team was so impressed by his performance in European championships that it offered him a $200,000, three-year contract, but he turned it down, preferring to remain in Zadar.

Kresimir has a subtle sense of humor that isn't totally translatable. As he listens and talks, even as he plays basketball, there is a mischievous smile playing at the corners of his mouth. He values his personal privacy very highly, and when he's asked a personal question, he often gives a humorous answer that's just plausible enough to make you wonder.

His English, like his basketball, is unorthodox but effective. In combination with his drowsy Yugoslavian accent, it always seems perfectly correct, for him at least.

You can't watch Kresimir play ball without knowing that he loves it. He grins when he's happy, grimaces when he's not, and hams it up all over the floor. Put Kresimir Cosic and a crowd of basketball fans together, and you've got instant magic. We looked him up when he was in Salt Lake City on a visit and asked him a few questions.

Q. You surprised a lot of people when you joined the Church. Could you tell us something about your conversion?

Kresimir: I had never heard about the Church before I came here. In Yugoslavia most of the young people are completely atheistic, and that's the way I lived. When I came to Provo I didn't change. I was an atheist for two years while I was in Provo. Nobody was farther from becoming a Mormon than I was. I just lived my way, and people lived their way. I obeyed all the rules of BYU, tried to be as good as I could, and tried to play ball and do my studying and other things. When I was a junior, I decided to figure out a few things.

I didn't decide to join the Church because of any one thing. There were some things that I wanted to know. I had a few questions that no one could answer. It just happened. We as Mormons believe in personal things everyone can know by himself. It all depends on how badly you want to know something. That's the whole point. If you have a desire in the Church to know something, you can know it; there's no question about that. If something is really bothering you, you probably go to somebody for advice. If it's football you want to know about—what kind of a play you are going to play—you can ask me, and I don't have any idea. I just can't help. It's the same if you're going to the wrong church. They can't give you an answer. So you ask, and find out, and you join the true church. So I just decided to join the Church.

Q. I've heard that the Book of Mormon impressed you

very much when you were studying the Church. Is this true?

Kresimir: Of course. You just read the book and want to get baptized—and that's it.

Q. Who gave you the book?

Kresimir: You can buy those books for fifty cents.

Q. What impressed you about the Book of Mormon?

Kresimir: Well, it's certainly the best book I have ever read. There's no question about that. The book applies to to-day's people much more than in the days when Joseph Smith translated it, because it speaks about the way it is now. I was traveling all over the world, and I saw many places, and I saw most of the prophecies being fulfilled; it's amazing. That really is a good book. There are many things in it that are coming true now.

Q. Were your friends in Yugoslavia surprised when they learned you had joined the Church?

Kresimir: You bet they were surprised. That's the last thing they thought was going to happen.

Q. You are a national hero. Has your popularity suffered since you joined the Church? Do people think you are strange or weird?

Kresimir: Almost everyone thinks I'm crazy anyway, so that's nothing new. As far as popularity goes, I just live my life normally and play because I have fun. Now people know I'm a Mormon. Some of them don't think becoming a Mormon was too smart a thing to do—most of them don't— but they just have to take me that way, and that's it.

Q. Have you been happier since becoming a member of the Church?

Kresimir: Of course. And if I hadn't known I would be, I wouldn't have been baptized.

Q. I've heard that while you were at the BYU you spent quite a bit of time speaking to firesides and other youth groups.

Kresimir: When I was baptized I changed completely. It's a completely different story to be a Mormon and a non-Mormon. I didn't like to speak in public, but I got to think-ing later on, "I have to." There are some things we've got to help others with; it doesn't make any difference if we like it or not. I like to live and I like to have fun. It was kind of uncomfortable to have to speak all the time. But it was okay, if people wanted to hear me. I told them what I thought, not what they wanted to hear.

Q. Speaking of fun, have you found that joining the Church has interfered with your having fun?

Kresimir: I think that's really the best part, because you can really have much more fun. I really believe that living the gospel is fun, but it is hard. It's not hard to play with a team if you can just sit on the bench, if you don't have to practice or anything. But if you've got to participate all the time, then it's kind of difficult. But I don't think it's worthwhile to ask if there is any sacrifice. There's no sacrifice at all. You don't sacrifice anything when you invest five cents and receive a thousand dollars in return.

Q. I've heard that you're quite a student of the scriptures. Is this true?

Kresimir: No, I just read normally. I believe that the scriptures are the best part of literature, so why not read them? I used to spend hours reading magazines, just to pass the time. Or I played cards for days and days and nights and nights, and I smoked and drank and all those things—just to pass the time! I still like to read magazines or do things just to pass the time, but most of the time, it's stupid to just let it pass. Of course, I'm not telling anybody else how to spend his time.

Q. What have you learned from your world travels?

Kresimir: I have a chance to talk to people. The gospel really teaches us to try. I have to meet people, really get acquainted—and I've found I can enjoy the way different people live.

New Era, February 1974, p. 9. Used by permission of the authors.

My friend
and next-door neighbor   Clark W. P. Larkins

My friend and next-door neighbor in New Zealand had, unbeknown to me, been watching my family's attitudes, behavior, and various other peculiarities that are quite normal among Saints, but appear unique to nonmembers. He has mentioned since our high dress standards and our close family life.

I remember mentioning the Church during a back-fence conversation, but he immediately let me know that he wasn't interested. That was in May 1974. About six months later his barriers had been broken down a little, and we conversed quite freely about the Church principles and doctrines. About that time his wife became ill and was hospitalized for three weeks. When she returned home we asked if we could help in any way. He replied firmly that he preferred to be independent, and that he could manage alone. Two days later my wife called at their home while the husband was at work, and she could see that the wife was really more ill than the husband had known. My wife immediately took her to the hospital, where she remained for ten days.

On December 14, 1974, just after my neighbor's wife returned from the hospital, missionaries from our ward called upon them. After one lesson, there was a deep change in the husband's attitude. The missionaries asked if they could give the wife a blessing, and he agreed. The Holy Ghost truly bore witness to this couple that day, and they agreed to be baptized as soon as the wife was well enough. The date was set for December 21. Many persons in the neighborhood and ward were excited and planned to attend the baptismal service.

Then, on December 20, we received heartbreaking news. The wife had died that morning from a brain tumor, leaving her husband and five children. The news of her passing was tragic to her family, but it was heartwarming to see the Saints rally around and comfort them.

The immediate thoughts were to postpone the baptism

for at least a few weeks. But the husband wished to continue with their plans, and he and four of their children (the fifth was under eight years of age) were baptized as scheduled in a very spiritual and emotional meeting. That Sunday a special family service was held at their home, and on Monday a filled chapel greeted the funeral cortege. There we saw the husband and his children bid farewell to their beloved wife and mother with hearts filled not only with sorrow, but also with happiness. They possessed a newfound knowledge of where they came from, why they are here, and where they are going.

Today my neighbor is president of the ward Sunday School and holds the Melchizedek Priesthood. One of his sons is a teacher and another a deacon. December of 1975 was a memorable month for the family, because they were sealed for time and all eternity in the temple.

However, the story does not end there. As mentioned before, members of the ward all rallied around to help ease the burden of this family, taking care of their spiritual needs as well as their physical needs. This compassionate service was particularly noticed by nonmember relatives of the family. One sister in particular was especially moved by the love and concern of the Mormons—so much so that when missionaries in her hometown visited her, she was receptive to their message. A spiritual person by nature, she had long had a desire to find the truth, and her thirst for the truth had not been satisfied until she met with the missionaries.

She decided to move to our town and find work there as a schoolteacher. She began attending our ward, where she and her family were welcomed and fellowshiped by members and missionaries. Many bore testimony to her. Here at last she found the truth and knowledge for which she had been searching. After a particularly moving Sunday School lesson on the subject of the lost sheep, she decided that she and her eight-year-old daughter would be baptized and her smaller daughters would be blessed. Two weeks later she was called to serve as Primary chorister.

The conversion of these two choice families has been a

moving experience for me and my family; indeed, they are an inspiration to all members of our ward and stake. Now they too set the example for their nonmember friends, neighbors, and relatives.

"We talked by Vicki's incubator"

Vanessa J. Scholfield

*T*he last thing on my mind as I settled into my new surroundings was religion. I was a live-each-day-as-it-comes type of person and avoided such subjects as religion and politics. I had just returned from an exciting five months in Israel, still wanting to talk about it whenever I could, wistfully thinking of the all-too-easy time I had there. I could have stayed, but the desire to travel further was greater, so some money had to be earned.

In April 1973 I arrived on the Isle of Man in the British Isles. I was to work at the only pediatric unit there, a somewhat old-fashioned unit, but it would serve my purpose. After all, I wasn't going to get involved with the people around me, so it didn't really matter what the place was like.

Once into the working routine, I was told that a very sick baby was returning to the unit from the mainland, to spend her last days near her home. She wasn't expected to live more than a few months, and perhaps only a few weeks.

I was off work the day Vicki arrived. On returning to work, I was taken to see her. She was only a scrap of a thing—all bones, big blue eyes, and gingery-colored hair. She was just about holding her own with the help of oxygen and humidity. She was fed through a tube, since she was far too weak to suck; breathing was just about all she could manage.

That evening, as the senior nurse, I attended to Vicki while the juniors coped with the rest of the children. As I approached the incubator, I noticed a small woman sitting beside the incubator, obviously Vicki's mother, Mrs. Corllett.

We exchanged polite greetings, as I assessed the situation. I didn't know what mental state she would be in, after having learned of her baby's serious condition. Also, it wasn't the first time she had been in the pediatric unit; her first baby had died when two days old, and her second died at two and a half years from leukemia. Here she was a third time, and I wondered how she was going to react; I knew

65

also that she had a two-year-old toddler and husband at home who needed to be cared for.

She came nearer as I fed Vicki, and I could see that she was a tiny woman. Our eyes met over the incubator, and a strange feeling coursed through me. As we talked, our conversation polite but not stilted, I wondered, Was she in complete control of her feelings? Or did she know something that I didn't know? I had to find out. Here her baby was at death's door, according to the doctors, and yet Mrs. Corllett was able to show concern for others. It wasn't a false, detached attitude; it was genuine love. How did she do it?

Fortunately the unit was going through a quiet spell. We weren't admitting any children because of a recent measles case; we had to wait fourteen days to be sure there was no contagion. During this time I had plenty of time to talk to Mrs. Corllett, plenty of time to learn about her and for her to learn about me. She was a good listener, and so I told her about my recent travels and all that I planned to do in the future. She seemed to understand so much about me, but I was still a little puzzled by her.

The fact that she was a Mormon came to light one day as I spied a copy of the Book of Mormon under Vicki's incubator. She had refused my offers of tea and coffee previously, but I hadn't known why. In just six days I had become so drawn to her that I asked if I might attend Vicki's blessing. The mission president was coming over from Ireland to perform it, and I was curious to see what went on. But it wasn't just curiosity that made me ask; I felt almost a magnetic force drawing me ever closer to Vicki and her mother.

This feeling was unusual for me. As a rule I never allow myself to become involved with our patients and their parents apart from what is necessary while doing my job.

Still feeling confused, I attended Vicki's blessing. Despite her critical condition, we allowed her mother to dress her in a beautiful white dress and wrap her in a shawl. Then the mission president and elders arrived. They gently took Vicki from her mother, held her tenderly, and placed their hands upon her. The voice of the mission president, as he gave the blessing, was so full of love and sincerity that something stirred within me again, much stronger this time.

I wouldn't allow myself to cry; that would have been too embarrassing and a show of weakness. Instead I held inside me all that I felt. I felt Mrs. Corllett's eyes on me; she seemed to sense what was happening.

After the blessing the group stayed to talk for a while. I can't recall anything specific—only that I could feel barriers within me breaking down. Listening to Mrs. Corllett in particular stirred the inner me that had been subdued for so long.

Still unsure of where all this was going to lead, I started going to her home. She seemed so aware of my needs and wasn't at all inhibited about expressing her feelings for me, her family, her fellow church members, and her friends who weren't Mormons. Yet I wouldn't let the last barrier drop; I wouldn't say, "I want to take the discussions." I felt that I had to be sure of my motives. It seemed such a big step to take, and I wasn't sure I could cope with a very different way of life.

Mrs. Corllett, whom I now called Violet, was patient in answering all my questions, supporting me, and encouraging me by telling me to take just one step at a time instead of trying to accomplish everything at once. Part of me knew that what she was saying was true, but the rest of me held on to what had been the only way of life for me—complete independence.

One evening she asked if I was completely happy. Was I? Suddenly I found myself crying until I could cry no more, such sweet release from weeks of torment. Then, as if that wasn't enough, Violet told me that until I had the gift of the Holy Ghost and his companionship and strength, Satan would still try to take me back. She was right; Satan certainly tried. There were times when I dreaded seeing Violet because I knew she was right—and I wasn't sure I had the strength to resist much longer.

The more Violet shared her beliefs and life-style with

me, the more I could see Vicki thriving. I just knew that this was the way of life I had been searching for, and that Vicki wasn't going home until I was safely home—safely in the true church of our Heavenly Father.

And so I began to meet with the missionaries, and I finally agreed to set a date for baptism. Then I went home for a short vacation with my family. I couldn't tell them—I wasn't strong enough to be able to handle their comments and questions. I tried to talk to a girl friend but found I couldn't. I wanted her to share this newfound joy, but somehow my approach was all wrong.

Violet met me at the airport on my return to the island. I was still utterly confused, but she allayed my fears. I felt a new surge of strength to make the last hurdle home.

At precisely 4:30 P.M. on June 2, 1975, I was baptized at a small beach on the Isle of Man. It was a gray, cold day, yet as I strode from the water, I literally glowed. I was confirmed and given the gift of the Holy Ghost the following day in fast and testimony meeting. I had taken the first steps to returning to my Heavenly Father in the celestial kingdom.

Each day I grow and learn a little more of what is expected of me as a Latter-day Saint. On November 1, 1975, I began serving a health mission. I feel I have come a very long way from that cold, gray day in June 1973 when I met the Corlletts. I pray that I will be a means of bringing many souls into The Church of Jesus Christ of Latter-day Saints.

"The most glorious Being my eyes have ever beheld"

Melvin J. Ballard

I bear witness to you that I know that the Lord lives. I know that he has made this sacrifice and this atonement. He has given me a foretaste of these things.

I recall an experience which I had two years ago. . . . On the Fort Peck Reservation where I was doing missionary work with some of our brethren, laboring among the Indians, seeking the Lord for light to decide certain matters pertaining to our work there, and receiving a witness from him that we were doing things according to his will, I found myself one evening in the dreams of the night in that sacred building, the temple. After a season of prayer and rejoicing I was informed that I should have the privilege of entering into one of those rooms, to meet a glorious Personage, and as I entered the door, I saw, seated on a raised platform, the most glorious Being my eyes have ever beheld or that I ever conceived existed in all the eternal worlds. As I approached to be introduced, he arose and stepped towards me with extended arms, and he smiled as he softly spoke my name. If I shall live to be a million years old, I shall never forget that smile. He took me into his arms and kissed me, pressed me to his bosom, and blessed me, until the marrow of my bones seemed to melt! When he had finished, I knelt at his feet, and, as I bathed them with my tears and kisses, I saw the prints of the nails in the feet of the Redeemer of the world. The feeling that I had in the presence of him who hath all things in his hands, to have his love, his affection, and his blessing was such that if I ever can receive that of which I had but a foretaste, I would give all that I am, all that I ever hope to be, to feel what I then felt.

Bryant S. Hinckley, *Sermons and Missionary Service of Melvin J. Ballard* (Deseret Book Co., 1949), pp. 155-56.

By your pupils you'll be taught

Patricia Lett

When I was a teenager our family lived for two years in Chicago, Illinois, where we had the experience of a lifetime—the opportunity to do missionary work. It was like a two-year mission for the whole family. While there we were able to see how the Church changes lives and the joy our friends found in doing what they knew to be true. The following is the testimony of a schoolteacher after she was converted to the gospel.

*M*y testimony of the Church is a growing one. New chapters are continually being added and will be as long as I am a member.

In July 1966 my son and I were in a serious automobile accident. It was a miracle that we survived. I spent the next few years wondering why we had been spared, feeling that we must still have something worthwhile to accomplish. I spent much time in studying, reading, and praying, hoping to find the answer.

I had been teaching at the Anne Sullivan School in Prospect Heights, Illinois, for four years when Carol Burr enrolled in my class. In the twenty-three years I have been teaching I have learned much from my pupils, but nothing has ever equaled the lesson I was to learn from Carol and her family.

One day last spring Carol put a book on my desk and asked if I would like to read it.

"Fine, Carol, I'll be happy to read it," I said.

Since school was closing soon and I had many things to do, I forgot all about the book. But Carol didn't. It wasn't long before I heard a little voice saying, "Mrs. Lett, have you read my book? I hope so, because I have to pack."

I did read it, and since it was volume one of a book of children's stories from the Book of Mormon, I asked Carol if I might borrow the second volume.

"The others are packed," she said, "but I have another book you can read."

Sure enough, the next day she presented me with a copy of the Book of Mormon. A few days later I heard the little voice again. "Mrs. Lett, would you like to meet some people from our church?"

"Oh, fine, Carol. It would be nice to meet someone sometime from your church." I didn't know what this statement would lead to, but I soon found out!

"Mrs. Lett, what day would be good for you to meet someone from my church?"

"Oh, make it Friday. That's as good a day as any, since I have no other meetings."

The next Friday Elders Grassley and Lott were at my classroom door ten minutes before the class was over. They met with me several times at school, and I was anxious to hear more. When the school year was over, we had to complete the missionary discussions in my home. After the sixth lesson Elder Grassley told me I was ready.

"Ready for what?" I asked.

Then he explained that he meant ready for baptism. I told him that there was still too much I didn't know about the Church. He replied that I would learn after I was a member. And this is true, for I am still learning, though it's now been some time since my baptism.

Last week my son was baptized and confirmed a member of the Church. I hope to see him marry in the temple and rear his children as fine, upstanding Latter-day Saints. If all this happens it will be because a child wanted to teach her teacher and wouldn't take no for an answer. Being a member of the true church, she knew that a child is as much a missionary as anyone.

A huge sack of flour

William R. Palmer

*T*he Spendlove family was very poor, as most pioneer families were. When the father was called on a mission, the family went to live with Sister Spendlove's mother. She spent much time worrying about earning enough money to send to her husband on his mission, but when the time came there was always enough.

Time passed, and the father would be released in the fall. Sister Spendlove decided to go back to their home in Tropic, Utah, to prepare for his return. It was much harder than she had imagined. The day came when the food supply ran out. The only thing they could do was to pray as a family and individually. She was working on a dress for a neighbor and vowed to have it finished by morning so she could be paid and buy food for breakfast, but she was very weary.

Suddenly there was a knock on the door. A brother from down the road had brought her a huge sack of flour that he owed her. She said to him, "You don't owe me any flour."

To this he replied, "Oh, yes I do. I owe every missionary's wife a sack of flour."

Instructor, July 1953, p. 206.

*B*eing from Colombia, a country where the main desire of most of the people is to serve the state church, I was raised in a religious environment. Since I was very young it had been my desire to become a priest, and I tried in every way possible to convince my family that I should be allowed to become a priest. I was the third boy of a family of five, and it is the custom in most families in Colombia to dedicate the oldest son to the church. My oldest brother served in a seminary for seven years but left the seminary to get married. Because of the disappointment that my oldest brother had caused the family, they were not easily persuaded that I should enter the seminary, but I finally convinced them. I promised my father that I would not disappoint him as had my brother, and in 1963 I entered the seminary with a great desire to become a dedicated priest.

One day I was going to send a letter to Germany, and at the post office I found a nice card on one of the counters; it attracted my attention because it had a picture of a temple on it. I did not read the card but took it and put it in my pocket as I walked away from the post office. Two or three days later, as I was about to send my suit to the dry cleaner, I searched in my pockets to see if anything should be removed, and there in one of my pockets I found the card. I decided to keep the card, as it was attractive, and I read it in its entirety. After reading it I said to myself, "These people must be crazy to believe things like this."

An inscription on the card read LDS Los Angeles Temple, and two addresses were listed, one in South America and one in the USA. I had read that LDS is the same thing as Mormon, so I told myself, "I won't find out more—they are the polygamists with five or ten wives at the same time."

The next day I decided to write to the Andes Mission, since the Article of Faith about the Book of Mormon impressed me. I wanted to know what that book was about. I sent the letter off and went back to the seminary, where I quickly forgot the whole matter.

One day my sister came to visit me, and she gave me a letter and a little package from Peru. I opened it, and there was a Book of Mormon. The letter stated that presently there were no missionaries in Colombia, but if I wanted to learn more, as soon as Colombia was opened for their labors the missionaries would visit me. The letter contained a challenge that I read the Book of Mormon. When my sister quizzed me about the letter, I told her it was a letter from a friend, and I didn't open the package until she had left.

I do not know why, but I started to read the book. Even during my study time I read it, covering it with my Bible. I read up to Mosiah in four days.

In July my sister visited me again and said that some Americans had called at my house and asked for me. I was surprised, for I did not know any Americans and had forgotten about the book. However, I told my sister that if they returned, she was to give them my telephone number. A few days later they called me. They said they were Mormon missionaries and wanted to talk to me. I told them that I was in a seminary and it would be difficult to arrange a visit. However, they insisted, and it was arranged for them to visit me the next day. I cautioned them to say that they were just friends, not missionaries, when they came to visit. They did, and they were able to talk with me. I was impressed after the first discussion, but I told them, "I shall never change from my church. I know it is true, and I want to be a priest." The missionaries exhorted me to read the Book of Mormon and to pray. I was afraid to pray. I believed at that time that my church was true, and I sincerely desired to become a priest.

I do not know why, but I continued to read the Book of Mormon. By the time the missionaries returned to visit me three or four days later, I was reading in Moroni. They gave me a second lesson and I was most impressed.

One afternoon I slipped away from the seminary and went to an LDS meeting. The membership in attendance was small, but I enjoyed the talks.

The visits by the missionaries continued. When we reached the lesson on faith, they asked me if I would be baptized, but I replied, "All I really wanted to know was more about the Mormons." They were a little discouraged, I think, but again exhorted me to pray and to continue reading the Book of Mormon. They didn't make another appointment. I told them I would call if I wanted to know more, and again I told them I wanted to become a priest in my church.

The next morning I awoke with the realization that I had a testimony. I immediately telephoned the missionaries and made an appointment for them to see me. During the sixth discussion I told them that I was underage and that my family expected me to become a priest; I knew it would be difficult to secure written permission from my father. I gave the missionaries the address of my father's office. When they went to visit him, he thought they were joking when they said they wanted to baptize me. Then he realized they were serious, and he became very angry. He said that he would not care if I became Mormon, but if I did, I would have to look for a new home.

I was baptized in a very cold swimming pool on September 6, 1966.

My father forgave me, but he was opposed to my attending the Church.

I was called to be the branch clerk two weeks after my baptism, and it was quite a challenge for a sixteen-year-old boy. I was clerk for over two years. I even prepared my own membership record. I was one of the first members of the LDS Church in Colombia.

A year later my mother and my father died. I found that continuing my high school education was a hardship, and many times I was hungry and without money for necessities. My family was rich, but they would not give me anything because I was a Mormon.

Shortly after graduation I came to the United States and attended Ricks College in Rexburg, Idaho, where I had been given a full-tuition scholarship.

I had the privilege of being called on a mission to my

own country, and when I returned to Colombia as a missionary there were five thousand members. I labored there for two years. I learned to love my own people, and I made many wonderful friends. I was released from my mission in August 1973.

At the present time I am attending BYU. I have a testimony and I am truly convinced that this church is true and that Joseph Smith was a true prophet of God.

New Era, July 1974, p. 39. Used by permission of the author.

*B*oxing had a good foothold on the island of Niue Fekai in the South Pacific, where I spent my mission. There were more boxing gloves than washtubs. As a normal matter of course, when we went to the villages to conduct meetings, we would hold boxing clinics for the *fuatas* (young men).

One such trip to the village of Liku stands out as I look back over my missionary experiences. The natives had constructed an outdoor arena, lining the area with fallen coconut logs and fashioning a fence and sunshade by placing upright coconut branches around the outside of the logs. I entered the arena with the native boys clamoring to get involved.

This particular day I was going to teach them how to lead with a left jab and follow up with a right cross. I began by working with two of them, and as I had them sparring, I was attempting to help them understand the combination. Suddenly things came to a halt. I could not figure out why, but they seemed to lose interest. This was not natural, for the natives were real scrappers. It was then that a well-built stranger, who stood at the edge of the spectators, introduced himself. Speaking in the Niuean native tongue, he indicated that he was the village boxing champion.

With this local expert present, small wonder the native boys had lost interest in the instruction of the white man! I showed my pleasure at his presence by inviting him to come into the center of the arena and assist me in teaching the boys. He thrust his hands willingly into some boxing gloves offered to him and entered the ring. I had not noticed that while I had only stuffed the strings into my gloves and gripped the gloves to hold them on, the stranger had laced his securely. I indicated to him that we were learning the left jab to a right cross, and I would appreciate his assisting me. I told him and the natives sitting around the circle that I would throw a few left jabs; then I would watch until he shifted his guard to protect the right side of his face and, following, I would demonstrate the opening for the right cross.

I was going to pull the punch, so there would be no real contact other than was sufficient to make the point of the shifted guard. We began, and I retreated from the solid wall of leather that was thrown. I reiterated that we were merely sparring and were going to demonstrate to the boys the combination of left jab and right cross. Again we squared off, again the air was full of leather, and again I retreated.

I turned to Elder Mosese Muti, my Tongan missionary companion, and told him to lace my gloves. Then I returned to the center of the ring and again announced that we were going to demonstrate the left jab and right cross combination. With that the stranger charged. This time I was expecting it and covered until an opening came, then thrust a left jab to the right side of his face. He was not hit hard—just enough to let him know that I had penetrated his guard. We continued, and I was able to insert a series of left jabs, each penetrating and making contact.

None of the blows did more than establish the presence of a weakness in his protection. His guard had shifted to the right side of his face to ward off the left jabs. I mentioned this to the native boys who were watching, noting that he was shifting his guard and leaving an opening on his left side. Then I announced that I was going to thrust through a right cross, to demonstrate the presence of the shift of his guard. The stranger, who was listening to the whole narrative, did not connect it with the sequence of events, for he rushed forward just as I straightened out my right arm with the right cross. It connected squarely, his head popped back, and his eyes were rolling as he fell to the ground. We immediately helped him up to one of the seating logs and assisted him as he tried to clear his head.

As his eyes focused, he looked directly at me and said, *"To taha iloilo, kia fanogonogo ke he palagi na. Kua iloa a ia haana a tau kupu."* ("Listen to that white man. He knows what he is talking about.")

From that moment on we had no trouble with the natives in that village. They were friendly toward the missionaries.

We learned later that evening that the stranger was the village constable, which created great anxiety until he appeared and declared that *"Ko Eleta Tomosoni, Kua haaku a kapitiga."* ("Elder Thomson is my friend.")

The village constable would never come to our church meetings, but neither would he allow anyone from that village to create any disturbance for the missionaries nor allow anyone to cause the missionaries any grief.

Helvi Temiseva:
victor in a wheelchair

Paul C. Richards

*L*ike most of her young friends, Helvi Temiseva was excited about going to school. She was an intelligent, active child who skied, swam, played hide-and-seek, and enjoyed all the other things that children did in Hameenlinna, a small city in southern Finland about sixty miles from Helsinki. But little did she realize as she entered the first grade that this was to be her last full year of school for thirty-three years.

If she had known that, perhaps Helvi would have appreciated school more, but as it was, she was disappointed that first day because she already knew how to read while the rest of the children were just learning A of the alphabet. Finnish children start school at age seven, but Helvi wasn't one to wait that long for her education. She had used her older sister's schoolbooks to teach herself to read. There was to be much self-teaching in the next thirty-three years before she would finally reach college.

At age eight Helvi had an attack of polio. This kept her home during her second-grade year. But she read many things on her own, and when the time came, she was permitted to enter the third grade. She started with new hopes, but then the schools were closed because of the war. They opened again the next year, but Helvi's crippled condition kept her from attending full-time. However, she kept up on her studies and was planning to make a full year of it in the fifth grade. She was eleven and still had hopes of finishing her education, getting married someday, and rearing a family. Then her whole world fell apart.

It started with a fever and swollen, aching joints. A severe attack of rheumatoid arthritis affected every joint in her body. Now there would not even be swimming, the only sport that polio had left to her, or any of the other pleasures that most people take for granted. Even eating was a laborious, painful process.

Rheumatoid arthritis is an extremely painful, crippling disease that has no cure. Doctors can sometimes stop its progress in slow cases, but nothing could be done for Helvi. She was hit hard and fast, and all the doctors could do was try to alleviate the pain. The disease stiffens joints, making them almost like solid bone. Any movement of the fused joints results in agonizing pain, somewhat like the pain of a severely sprained ankle.

"All we can do is try to get the joints to stiffen in the best possible position," the doctors told Helvi's parents. "There is nothing else we can do."

Since then, Helvi has undergone seven major surgical operations on her joints to give some flexibility to her rigid, eighty-pound body. With difficulty and pain she can now be placed in a semi-sitting position and make limited use of her hands and arms. Other than being able to write, use an electric typewriter, feed herself, handle a telephone, and hold a book if it is placed on her lap, she is completely helpless and must have constant care.

Helvi knew well enough back then that she was terribly ill, but she didn't fully realize that there would never be a cure. She still had hopes there in her bed as she lay perfectly still day after day—first, three months at home and then three months in a Helsinki hospital. As the war intensified, arrangements were made to send Finnish children to Sweden where it was safer. Helvi also had to be moved. What a horrifying thought, especially for a twelve-year-old! She was to leave her country, her friends, her four brothers and one sister, and her parents, who had learned to take such delicate care of her. She was packed in cotton to make the agonizing journey by train.

During the three years Helvi spent in a Swedish hospital, she maintained her hopes for a cure. A former patient at the hospital had gone out, earned a college degree, and then come back to volunteer as a tutor for the children. She was one of the first of a long line of good Samaritans Helvi was to meet. She patiently taught Helvi the standard school subjects and gave her encouragement by reading poetry.

After the war Helvi returned home, speaking fluent Swedish and stumbling a little with her Finnish. She was fifteen now, old enough to fully understand that there would never be a cure. There were operations, grave-looking doctors slowly shaking their heads, and months on end of indoor confinement during the long Finnish winters.

She struggled just as other young people do to find her identity during those teen years, but in her case the struggling was more intense than for most. And yet all seemed so hopeless.

"My whole being agreed with the idea that we ought to do our best in the role given to us, but what was my role? Thus far I had been identified as patient number so-and-so to such a degree that I had almost lost my identity. I rebelled against the way people identified me with my wheelchair, but without a distinctive self-image I was unable to change the situation. I was nothing. Man cannot stand for long the thought of being nothing."

But at the end of those searching years Helvi found herself—and the gospel. She joined The Church of Jesus Christ of Latter-day Saints after she turned twenty-one. It took two missionaries to carry her into the cold waters of a Finnish lake for the baptismal service. Some of Helvi's family were opposed to her baptism, but this did not stop them from continuing to help her in every way possible. Her troubles had helped develop a strong bond of family love that continues to this day.

As Helvi studied the gospel, she says she was given a heaven-colored thought. "I realized that I was a daughter of the Almighty God, my Heavenly Father, and my role was an eternal one. I knew I had another background other than the bondage of my wheelchair, and I knew also that my life had a purpose. I took to heart the quotation that President David O. McKay used to repeat so often: 'Whate'er thou art, act well thy part.'

"We all strive along together, and the thing that counts is not who leaps farthest or who has the strongest legs, but rather if we help each other on the way, and if we have the strength to endure till the end."

Helvi vowed that if ever she was asked to do anything

for the Church, she would try her best. But what could she do when everything had to be done for her? Church was too far away to attend, and even if she could go, she could only sit helplessly in her special reclining wheelchair. The missionaries came to her home to visit and administer the sacrament, but that was about all the Church contact Helvi had. She continued studying on her own.

Then, six months after her baptism, Helvi's mission president, Henry A. Matis, asked her to do some translating for the Church. The only English she knew was what she had learned on her own, so the work was slow and tedious. Practically every other word had to be looked up in the dictionary. Helvi's first translation project had plenty of rough spots, but it showed she had what it took to do such work. She became more and more proficient and finally was given a regular job as a translator.

After several years she moved to Helsinki to be close to mission headquarters. Her widowed mother came along to provide the necessary daily care. Helvi started earning enough to pay rent and buy food with a little money left over for savings. It felt good to be somewhat self-sustaining after twenty years of supposed helplessness.

But then another problem arose. Helvi's mother became ill, and it looked as if Helvi would have to enter a home for the elderly where there would be no possibility of continuing her translation work. There was not enough money to hire anyone for the type of care she needed, and, as she says, "I had a real bad need." She prayed for help and soon another good Samaritan came on the scene. It was a young girl, a member of the Church, who was in Helsinki looking for work. She agreed to stay with Helvi for two weeks until someone else could be found. The girl, Anneli Ylanko, ended up staying two and a half years.

"Anneli was a very important person in my life. She would tell me, 'You haven't been living at all. We'll have to get some life into you.' She made new clothes for me and started taking me to church. I had never been to a regular meeting in an LDS chapel before. Anneli also took me to the first movie I had seen in twenty years. She was a real life-giving force in my life."

There were still discouraging times, such as after the operations, when Helvi was too weak to translate. There were a multitude of other problems that always accompany anyone in a wheelchair, but these didn't stop Helvi. She had now had a good taste of life and liked it.

As she was able, Helvi continued her work, doing all of the translating on a little lap board held in her wheelchair in her apartment. She had been working with President J. Malcolm Asplund, then head of the mission, on a translation of the Doctrine and Covenants. President Asplund returned home to Logan, Utah, before the project could be completed. Helvi's friends, knowing of her desire to travel, decided it would be good for her to go to Logan to finish the work.

Anneli accompanied her to the United States and provided care until a new good Samaritan could be arranged for. This time it was Marja-Liisa Joukama (now Gomis) who came to help Helvi.

"These people who look after me are truly good Samaritans," Helvi says. "I can't afford to pay them much, and the work they do is much more than an eight-hour-a-day job. They have to be with me on weekends and holidays, and I can't give them vacations. I can be alone for a few hours if they arrange everything on my lap, but that is all."

Marja-Liisa and others who have since traveled with Helvi have paid much of their own transportation costs.

Helvi stayed two years in the United States, finishing the Doctrine and Covenants project, doing genealogy work, traveling to California and Oregon to fulfill a lifelong dream of spending a winter in a warm climate, and visiting the Salt Lake, Logan, and Los Angeles temples. "I really enjoyed my life during those two years. It was the most active I have ever been since my childhood, and it was good," she recalls.

While in Utah, Helvi studied Hebrew at the Brigham Young University Salt Lake Center for Continuing Education. Her thirst for knowledge increased and prompted her to see about getting into college. But she had never graduated from high school.

She returned to Finland determined to earn her high school diploma, a degree that in Finland is equivalent to the sophomore level in American universities. She spent two years studying all the subjects taught in Finnish high schools. "I had no teachers, just books," she says.

In the spring of 1972 Helvi took the rigorous written and oral examinations required for graduation. She did well in all thirteen subjects.

That fall she returned to the United States and enrolled at Brigham Young University in Provo, where she is now a sophomore majoring in English. She is also studying Hebrew, Greek, and religion. In addition, she translates. Phileon B. Robinson, Jr., assistant dean of BYU's Division of Continuing Education, describes Helvi as a bright student who reads everything. "And she is one of the best translators in the Church," he adds.

There are still many problems to deal with, and fortunately, there are still good Samaritans around to help Helvi over the major obstacles. For instance, when Daryl Gibb, a former Finnish missionary and now a BYU faculty member in linguistics, heard that Helvi had to be pushed several miles each day in her wheelchair to get to school and back, he gave her his Volkswagen bus. He says simply, "My wife and I had the bus, we knew of Helvi's situation, we felt our obligation to do something, and we did it. We can't stand by and see people suffer, especially when they are trying their best to better themselves." Brother Gibb and his wife, Pirkko Niemi Gibb, a native of Finland, had to buy another car to replace the van, which had been their only means of transportation.

Others help too, like the friends who heard of Helvi's need for an electric typewriter. They went out and bought her a brand-new one. And when her companion's time came to return to Finland, Helvi's friend Marja-Liisa again volunteered to care for her—this in addition to her seven-month-old child. Marja-Liisa's husband, Jose Gomis, sometimes drives Helvi's van, but when he is at work, Helvi gets on the phone to seek help from others who have offered their services. It is not always easy, but as Helvi says, "Somehow we manage it, with God's help."

Helvi is a modest and sensitive person. Like many others who have accomplished great things in life, she does not fully realize the magnitude of her accomplishments. But she has done much. Who would expect an almost totally helpless arthritic to graduate from high school without the aid of teachers, to attend college, to speak several languages, to travel across oceans and continents, and to earn a living as a professional translator? Who would expect it in an age when so many with so much do so much less?

Her English professor has summed it all up by saying, "Helvi, what an inspiration you are!"

And what does Helvi say? Simply this: "All these things never would have happened to me if I had not found the gospel of Jesus Christ."

New Era, October 1973, p. 28. Used by permission of the author.

My new employee   Ken Morse

I'll begin my story when I was about fourteen years of age. I had grown up not knowing honesty, truth, morals, or God, in a home where all that was taught was things of no eternal value. I can remember arguments at the dinner table with my younger sister concerning right and wrong. During such disagreements I would say to my mother, "That's not right. It's not fair." I would usually lose, and I'd leave the table to go pout in my room. That would do no good, and I would come out later still sullen and upset. Sometimes my father would say to me, "Wait until you go in the navy." Thinking that the navy was something special, I enlisted.

During my few years in the service I found some lazy men with no ambition or enthusiasm. I was stationed aboard the U.S.S. *Enterprise* for a tour in Vietnam. The job I had was quite demanding. I had to know what aircraft in our squadron were in flying condition, whether or not all systems were working, on which missions the various systems were needed, and so forth. At this time we were bombing quite heavily, and I saw waste of supplies, men, and time.

Upon my release from active duty, I wanted to relax and travel, so off I went trying to find the land of tomorrow, where people were happy and life was carefree.

I traveled extensively throughout the United States and Canada and then stopped in Ohio to visit with my grandparents. One day I called my family in California, and my dad mentioned that there was a donut shop for sale near our home. He had been in the bakery business most of his life, and since I hadn't settled on a worthwhile occupation for myself yet, I told him to take my money and buy the shop.

I loved my family and had always wanted to be close to my dad, so I made big plans for us to work in the shop together. However, the day I took over the shop my grandfather died, and my dad left me on my own. I learned fast about the world of business.

After a few months I needed to hire some new employees. A man who came into the shop every day mentioned that his daughter was looking for a job, so I told him to have her come in.

I hired her, and within a week after starting to work, she began asking such questions as, "Why do you swear? Why do you drink? Don't you know that coffee is bad for you?" I tried to answer these questions but really couldn't. Then she started talking about the church she belonged to and said she wanted me to go with her. I told her no, but she persisted. She mentioned she wanted me to go to "institute." It sounded like a hospital! But I was touched by her concern. We talked many times about religion and God. Finally I agreed to attend institute, and I started taking the missionary discussions from the institute director.

I had never prayed before, but I began to enjoy it. The hardest part for me was believing in Jesus Christ, since as a Jew I had been taunted and ridiculed all my life, and over the years, I had almost begun to hate Christians. But somehow the truth broke through.

When I met my new employee's family for the first time, I was impressed with their warmhearted concern for others. I was impressed by the clean-cut youths at the institute, the dedication of the Mormons, the organization of the Church.

Three months after the first discussion, I was baptized. One year later my new employee and I were married and sealed for time and all eternity in the Oakland Temple.

I have held many positions in my short time in the Church. I have come to love all people with whom I've come in contact for the abilities and talents they possess and their spirit of love. I still make donuts, but I'm no longer searching for the lost page in my life. I have found that truth which remains the same yesterday, today, and forever. I know that the gospel of Jesus Christ is true. I know that we have a loving Father who watches over us and is concerned about each one of us.

"I felt as clean
and white as bond paper"   *Rick Keller*

I was a newly appointed senior companion in the Philippine Mission. The other missionaries in my area had a family prepared for baptism, and since the nearest district leader was five hundred miles away, it was my privilege and assignment to interview the family to determine their readiness and worthiness for baptism.

This was a very special family. The father, who had formerly taught in another faith and who was an expert on the scriptures, had gained a strong testimony of the gospel. He had borne witness to those in his former faith of the incorrectness of their doctrines and practices, and he had taught his Sunday lessons from lessons that the missionaries had taught him the previous week. He was not ashamed of the gospel of Jesus Christ, and he had a strong desire to change the hearts of his friends and loved ones.

His family followed his example and were all converted to the principles that the elders had taught them.

The last person I interviewed was his seventeen-year-old daughter. We went through the outlined questions, and tears began to flow down her cheeks as she asked forgiveness and counsel because she had transgressed God's laws. I said a silent prayer, asking for the Spirit to counsel me in my duty. I don't know how long the interview lasted, but our Heavenly Father was directing me, and the Spirit bore strong witness that she had followed the correct steps of repentance and was ready for baptism.

And so members of this wonderful family were baptized, confirmed, and given the gift of the Holy Ghost. That same day I received a telegram informing me that I was being transferred.

Several months later I returned to that area again to take care of some special business for the mission president. During my short visit, I attended sacrament meeting, where the father of that family was presented for receiving the priesthood.

At that meeting, the daughter gave a talk. She explained how burdened she had been before her interview for baptism. Then she told of the beautiful feeling she had had at the baptismal service, and what a beautiful morning it had been. When the elder took her by the hand and led her down into the water and uttered the prayer of baptism, she said, "I felt as clean and white as bond paper."

This experience strengthened my faith concerning the miracle of forgiveness in one's life.

A little boy gave them
the Book of Mormon

Rick Keller

My companion and I had been tracting for about a week in a new area where quite a few squatters had settled. A group of nearly fifty children had been following us all day long, and we were getting pretty tired and worn out. We hadn't had much success, but finally a man let us in to talk with him. We quieted the children down enough to give him our message and then made an appointment to come back in a few days to teach him and his family the first discussion.

When we returned for our appointment, we couldn't find the house, since they all looked the same to us. We asked the children where the family lived and they took us right to the door without any problems at all. I couldn't believe someone could find his way around that area.

We delivered our message of the restoration, bore our testimonies, and made an appointment to teach the plan of salvation. The family seemed to understand our message, though the wife couldn't express herself in English. Whenever we asked questions, she spoke in a Philippine dialect and her husband translated for us.

After the second discussion we asked them how they felt and what they understood about the Book of Mormon. The husband said he knew it was true. We asked his wife the same question. There was silence for a few seconds. Then she began to cry, and tears streamed down her cheeks. In her dialect, which her husband translated for us, she said that she knew the Book of Mormon was true. Just three days before our first visit a little boy had come into their home and had given them a copy of it. She expressed her love to us for coming to their home with the truth.

I don't think my companion and I stepped on the ground until the next day, we were so happy!

Many people might consider it a coincidence that a little boy had given these people the Book of Mormon, but I know better. Whatever is done in missionary work is never coincidence. It is a testimony to me to see how the Lord prepares people to accept the gospel.

This family has now been baptized, and they are on the path that leads to the kingdom of God. The little boy who gave them the Book of Mormon, whoever he was, prepared the way for us to teach them the gospel of Jesus Christ.

Work by the Spirit

South Korea is hot and humid in the summer and cold and wet in the winter. Although Seoul and some of the larger cities have modern conveniences, the towns and villages of the provinces do not offer much in the way of heating or cooling. The city of Chonju is near the center of the country in the heart of the rice belt. In July it is either rainy and humid or hot and dusty.

Elder Farnsworth and his companion were assigned to Chonju and had spent many weeks of hard labor during that summer. One very hot day they had a midafternoon appointment with the owner of a small inn. When they arrived at the inn, the owner was busy with one of his guests and said to the elders, "We will have to postpone our appointment for about forty-five minutes until I finish my business. There is a room with a fan and some easy chairs at the end of the hall. You look very tired and hot. Go there and rest, and I will be with you within the hour."

With sighs of relief the two missionaries started down the hall. Before they reached the room, Elder Farnsworth suddenly stopped and turned to his companion. "I have a feeling we should not waste this hour," he said. "We could place some Books of Mormon."

"I'm very tired and I know you are," his companion replied.

"Nevertheless, I remember the motto of our mission: 'Live by the Spirit, tract by the Spirit, work by the Spirit.' I believe the Spirit has spoken to me. Let's go."

After two unsuccessful tries at selling the Book of Mormon, they entered a small tailor shop and found a listening ear. The tailor bought a Book of Mormon. He listened to the discussions, and he and his family accepted the gospel and joined the Church.

Elder Farnsworth listened to the promptings of the Spirit, instead of resting. And another family has their opportunity for exaltation.

Two half-crown pieces   *John Nicholson*

*T*he following incident may serve to show that the hand of the Lord can be seen in the small events of life as well as the great ones.

In 1863, I was serving as a missionary in one of the northern counties of England. While trying with all my might to preach the gospel to investigators and to counsel and comfort the Saints in my field of labor, I received many manifestations of the goodness of God in guiding me in the course I should take.

One of the families of Saints I sometimes visited was very poor. While in bed one night, I dreamed that I was in this family's home and they were in great distress. The mother was in tears, and the children were also very upset. I knew at once that the cause of it all was that they had nothing to eat. I had two half-crown pieces in my pocket. I took them from my purse and handed them to the mistress of the house.

In the morning when I awoke, my dream was visibly impressed on my mind, and I decided to visit the family soon. Some appointments took me to another part of the town in the forenoon, and the impression left my mind for a few hours. I was about to enter a store to purchase a book when it came back to me. I put my hand into my pocket and found two half crowns. Instead of purchasing the book, I started for the home of this family. There the incidents of my dream were repeated in reality. The lady was in tears and the children were hungry and totally without food. My two half-crown pieces were, of course, handed over as in the dream.

Juvenile Instructor, vol. 6 (1871), p. 171.

The change
in my father

Estela Ayala

*F*rom the time I was five years old until I was eighteen years old, our home life was unhappy. As the oldest of nine children, I felt it keenly when my mother and young brothers and sisters suffered from the savage temper of a drunken father. I often wondered, "What can I do to bring a little happiness into our home?"

When I was fourteen, someone told me that one of the commandments of God was to honor your parents. Greatly interested, I asked, "How can I honor my parents?" I was told to study and become a good student, and that would please my parents; thus, I would be keeping a commandment by being a good student. I thought, "Now maybe I can bring a little happiness into our home." I studied to become the best student in the class and decided, by my behavior, to become the best daughter in town. Everyone respected and loved me for this, but nothing changed at home.

Thinking there must be something more I could do, I asked for another commandment of God and was told, "Love your neighbor as yourself." So I began working in a hospital where I could serve the sick, some of whom were very poor, and I came to feel a special love for all of them. I was happy in fulfilling this commandment, but still nothing changed at home. To make matters worse, my brother began to smoke and drink, and he would take no advice from me.

By this time I was eighteen, and it seemed all my efforts had been in vain. Still I had faith in God and didn't become discouraged. I felt that there was something more I could do.

Soon I left home to undertake some special studies. I thought about my family all the time. Twenty-two days later I went home to visit, and my mother was crying when she met me. I thought something terrible had happened, but she hugged me and said, "Since you went away, your father hasn't had anything to drink."

How happy I was! My father hugged me, and when we went into the house my mother said that the night I left, some Mormon missionaries had come. "Your father has read almost the whole Book of Mormon and is going to be baptized," she said. I was amazed.

My father had become like a little child. I could see repentance and humility in his eyes. He had changed completely. He had given up smoking and drinking and tried to keep the commandments the missionaries taught him. He treated me like a queen, and he treated my mother and brothers and sisters like royalty.

As a result our whole family was baptized—my parents and the five children who were old enough, including myself. My father, at age forty, became the best father in the world with a special humility, and my brother will soon serve as a missionary. What more could one ask? I know that my sacrifices were not in vain, and I know that the gospel of Jesus Christ has made our home one of the happiest in the world.

Ensign, February 1975, p. 42. Used by permission of the author.

A story
of conversion

Dean A. Peterson

*O*ne evening in 1964, when I was presiding over the Norway Mission, a knock came at the door of the mission home in Oslo. My son, Erlend, answered the door, and there stood a lovely young lady about nineteen years of age. She introduced herself as Solveig Laervik from South Africa, and asked if this were the headquarters for the Mormon Church in Norway. When Erlend answered in the affirmative, she said, "I want to be baptized."

This was an unusual and delightful surprise. Erlend invited her into our living room and introduced her to my wife and me. I asked her why she wanted to become a member of the Church and where she had learned about the gospel. She then related the following story.

Her mother was British and her father Norwegian. The family lived in South Africa, and she and her mother were on vacation and had been visiting with an uncle and aunt for a few weeks in Stavanger, on the west coast of Norway. Shortly after they arrived, two young American men came to the house. Her aunt answered the door and, after a moment, said to them, "Just a minute and I'll get someone who can speak English with you." She got Solveig, who visited with the young men for about half an hour. They told her of the great and important message of the restoration and bore their testimonies to her. They showed her a copy of the Book of Mormon, told her about it, and asked if she would like to read it. She was impressed by their message, sincerity, and enthusiasm. She replied, "Yes, I would like to read the Book of Mormon, but I do not read Norwegian."

One of the elders said to her, "I have recently come to Norway, and I brought some English copies of the Book of Mormon. I'll be happy to give one of them to you."

When her uncle returned home that evening, Solveig showed him her newly acquired book. He was a Lutheran minister, and upon seeing the Book of Mormon, he told Solveig not to read it, but to get rid of it at once. He said it was a false, evil, and abominable book. His tirade against it caused Solveig to have an increased desire to read it. She hid the book under the mattress in her bedroom and spent many hours studying it.

Solveig followed Moroni's admonition to ponder the things she read and to ask God, the Eternal Father, in the name of Christ, if they were not true; and she received a witness by the power of the Holy Ghost that they were true. (See Moroni 10:3-5.) She decided that when she and her mother left Stavanger, she would look up the Mormon Church and ask to be baptized.

During the week Solveig was in Oslo, Erlend and another elder gave her the missionary discussions. The week was happily concluded by her being baptized and confirmed a member of the Church. Solveig's mother had not objected to the baptism, but just before they were to leave Oslo for their home in South Africa, Solveig received a letter from her father stating that he had found a new Lutheran chapel and looked forward to the family attending meetings there. Solveig asked me how she could tell her father she had been baptized without his being terribly upset. I asked for his address and told her I would contact the mission president in South Africa at once and have him send missionaries to visit her father. By the time Solveig and her mother arrived home, missionaries had visited her father and he was taking the discussions.

Our daughter, Susan, who is about the same age as Solveig, corresponded with her and kept us informed of Solveig's activities in the Church. But when Susan married and moved away a couple of years after we returned home, we lost contact with Solveig.

One summer we received a letter from my former first counselor, Arne Bakken, telling us about the annual temple excursion of the Norwegian Saints to the London Temple. He said that a young woman and a young man from South Africa were married in the temple while the Norwegian Saints were there. The woman had previously been baptized in Norway, and she sent her regards to us.

In the summer of 1975, we received a call from Solveig. She was in Salt Lake City with her husband, Chris Robb, and their four little daughters. They had recently moved from South Africa to Alberta, Canada, and were on a visit to Utah. We invited them to come to Provo to stay with us for a visit and go with us to the Provo Temple. Our joy was great to renew acquaintance with Solveig, to learn of her happy life since joining the Church, and to meet her wonderful husband and children. We felt their great love for each other and their complete dedication to the gospel and the Church.

Solveig said her parents had nearly joined the Church a few years ago, but their well-meaning friends had discouraged it. She hopes and prays her parents will yet know the truth and have the courage to accept it.

Voyage on the ship International

William G. Hartley

*I*t was a calm night in the North Atlantic, but Captain David Brown awoke with a start. What a strange dream! His ship's crew, the mates, and even he himself, were all being baptized into the Mormon faith! What did it mean? And why had the dream occurred right after he had fallen asleep while kneeling in prayer? He arose and got into bed, pondering both this strange experience and the singular spirit of the Mormon company then aboard his ship, the *International.*

When the large sailing vessel was tugged oceanward into the Mersey River from Liverpool on February 25, 1853, she carried on board a Latter-day Saint emigrant company of 425, including a number of unbaptized friends and relatives, plus crew of twenty-six. Hail and snow pelted the ship as it anchored in the Mersey awaiting fair winds. Below deck Christopher Arthur, the fifty-six-year-old president of the company, divided the passengers into eight wards, each with a presiding elder assisted by a priest or teacher. Of the identifiable passengers there were 309 adults, 100 children, and nine infants.

Three days later Captain Brown decided to set sail into the Irish channel and begin the 5,000-mile voyage despite strong gales, heavy seas, sightings of storm-wrecked vessels, and spreading seasickness. The Saints steeled themselves for a long and hazardous venture, hoping that in five or six weeks they would safely disembark in New Orleans. By September they should reach Utah.

During the first Sabbath at sea, three Mormon meetings were held, open to everyone on board. Captain Brown, his mates, and the entire *International* crew attended the afternoon sacrament meeting. The captain, congenial and God-fearing, won the respect of the emigrants early in the journey.

Later in the week, violent Atlantic storms threatened to capsize the wooden vessel. One diarist noted that on March 10 a "strong gale [blew] from the east for five hours—ship rolling tremendously—sea like mountains on each side of the ship. Most of the luggage on the larboard side broke their lashing and rolled to the center of the steerage."

This crisis caused the priesthood to gather below deck, where they supplicated God to still the waves. Almost immediately Captain Brown came down to announce a sudden improvement in the weather. The hatches were again opened. But that night the *International* sailed into an even worse tempest. "Again our boxes were knocked about," wrote one, "and many of our pots and tins were smashed, and many articles lost." The scene was even more terrifying than on the preceding night. No cooking fires were allowed, and women and children could not leave their berths. For nearly fifteen hours the storm raged. Finally, about mid-afternoon the next day, the weather had eased enough so that the hatches could be reopened. It was that night, after having seen his ship safely through two days of near disaster, that the exhausted Captain fell asleep while praying and had his remarkable dream.

The voyage progressed. Despite the difficult beginning the emigrant company retained a continuing good spirit, particularly evident in their nightly and Sabbath day meetings. Speaking in tongues and prophesying were not uncommon. After four weeks at sea, the presiding elders reported all in their wards "to be in good standing, no sickness, quarreling, nor complaints of any kind." But they knew the ship was not making proper progress, averaging less than eighty miles per day against the troublesome head winds. On Easter Sunday, March 27, the Mormons fasted until late afternoon in thanksgiving to God for their preservation and in prayer for fair winds and smooth seas.

Captain Brown was likewise concerned about the turbulent sailing conditions. In four weeks, only one-third of the distance to New Orleans had been covered; there were 2,900 miles yet to go. He ordered an inventory of food reserves, which proved to be adequate unless the unfavorable winds continued. In the midst of the company's anxiety, the Spirit brought them reassurance on March 29: "A tongue interpreted that we should have a speedier voyage than was anticipated, as the Lord was well pleased with our fasting and had heard our prayers."

Events of the next few days and nights, however, seemed to negate that prophecy. Storms struck again: "strong gale; great swell on the water; ship rolling very much; many of the passengers sick. . . . Things rolling about." Outside the elements were at war, but within, the Spirit was at work. After one preaching meeting where "Brother Finch gave a brief and lucid explanation of the first principles," five converts were baptized. On April 1, the unfavorable winds continued, but at a testimony meeting, which many sailors attended, three more baptisms occurred, including the ship's carpenter—the first crew member to convert. The next day found food rations reduced. That evening three more sailors and one passenger were baptized in the testimony meeting.

How is someone baptized aboard a sailing vessel? Sometimes large barrels filled with salt water or a platform improvised by the side of the ship were used. On the *International,* according to one who was baptized there, the ordinance was performed on deck "in a large round vat holding probably 2,000 gallons of water." Why the vat was on board one can only surmise. But filled with sea water, it served well as a convenient font.

On the first Sunday in April, five weeks from Liverpool and still not halfway to New Orleans, a special church meeting was held in the steerage. While the vessel was tossed on the heavy seas, many testimonies were borne. Then "a proposition was made that we should pray through our president for favorable winds." Unitedly, they petitioned for divine assistance, "when, remarkable to relate, the Lord almost immediately answered our prayers." Christopher Arthur, Jr., twenty-two years old and not yet a Mormon, later recalled the moment: "Prayer was offered on the 3rd of April for a fair wind which was answered while we were on our knees." There was one more squall that night, but from then on, ideal weather sped the vessel toward Florida. During the next three days, as the Saints rejoiced "that our prayer was heard," the *International* sailed as far as it had during the previous two weeks. Frequently the stretched sails carried the ship 220 miles per day.

The new turn of events made the Saints extra joyous as they celebrated the birthday of the Church in a day-long festival on April 6. A sacrament service and four marriages occupied the morning. Afternoon festivities included "prayer and praise," songs, speeches, recitations, and instrumental music. Next came a specially prepared meal, "a repast of every delicacy the ship could afford or pastry cooking could invent." Evening merriment included national dances, singing, recitations, and "skipping the light fantastic toe until a late hour." The day produced fellowship and delight for all on board, including the crew and their captain.

While the *International* sped west toward port, the Mormon ranks continued to grow as predicted in Captain Brown's dream. Just before the April 6 festival, the captain's cook was baptized. On April 8, President Arthur's sixteen-year-old daughter, Mary Ann, and a Negro crewman were baptized. The second mate, three sailors, and Christopher Arthur, Jr., were baptized the next day. As the *International* slipped between Cuba and Florida a week later, the first mate joined the Church, as did three sailors and one emigrant the next day. Even 110-degree heat on April 17 did not squelch the Spirit, for the Saints held "first-rate meetings during the whole day; in the evening the ship's carpenter, captain's cook, and two sailors bore testimony to the truth of the work."

Captain Brown's spirit was troubled as the conversions continued. Some of his feelings were revealed when he gave landing instructions on April 18 and confessed his attraction to Mormonism; "he had crossed the seas many times," one diarist reported in quoting him, "but never felt so happy with any people as he had with the Latter-day Saints." He added that "his pride prevented him from immediately becoming a saint but he felt he soon should join us and come to Great Salt Lake City." Following his remarks, two more passengers were baptized. At testimony meeting the next evening, six sailors bore testimony and afterwards one sailor was baptized.

Three days before the voyage ended, and as the blackness of night was just starting to lighten along the eastern horizon at 4:30 A.M., Captain David Brown was baptized by President Arthur. That evening he and two others were confirmed members of the Church. Then, as a fitting climax to the *International's* conversion story, the captain and the ship's carpenter were ordained as elders, the first and second mates became priests, and the cook a teacher. As part of this service, at which the captain, the carpenter, and several crewmen bore testimony, two more crewmen were the final baptisms aboard the ship.

At 5:00 P.M. on April 23, the *International* docked in New Orleans, completing a fifty-four-day trip. President Arthur was pleased with the conduct both of the Saints and of the ship's crew. In his official report to President Samuel W. Richards of the British Mission, he particularly praised the captain: "To his honor I can say that no man ever left Liverpool with a company of saints, more beloved by them, or who has been more friendly and social than he has been with us."

The report credited the workings of the Spirit, coupled with the Saints' exemplary conduct, for the remarkable number of conversions made on the high seas. He proudly wrote:

"I am glad to inform you, that we have baptized all on board except three persons [the steward and his wife, both staunch Catholics, and the third mate, 'a very wicked fellow'—]. We can number the captain, first and second mates, with eighteen of the crew, most of whom intend going right through to the valley. . . . The carpenter and eight of the seamen are Swedish, German, and Dutch. . . . The others baptized were friends of the brethren. The number baptized in all is forty-eight, since we left our native shores."

Captain David Brown's prophetic dream of six weeks earlier had been 94 percent accurate.

New Era, September 1973, p. 6. Used by permission of the Church Historical Department and the author.

I made
a commitment

Dale Z. Kirby

Most men listen to their barber talk while he cuts their hair, but Dale Z. Kirby won't sit still for a barber who won't listen to a friendly explanation of the gospel.

Elder Kirby, director of the Saratoga (California) Institute of Religion, rarely, if ever, misses a chance to tell the interested about the Church.

When a bank officer who was opening the checking account for the institute asked, "What is this Church of the Latter-day Saints?," Elder Kirby was all set to go and soon had most of the bank personnel reading tracts and the Book of Mormon. He referred his real estate agent, the man who installed his telephone, and a furniture repairman to the missionaries.

One young man told Elder Kirby he wanted to learn of the gospel, but his schedule was so tight that the only time he could listen was at 5:00 A.M. on Wednesdays. Elder Kirby was never late for his early appointment.

This effort has paid off well. In the past two years he has brought more than two dozen people into the Church and has been involved in the conversion of many more people.

Through his encouragement and example, several institute students in their twenties who had earlier decided not to go on missions have seen the importance of this work and are now in the field as full-time missionaries.

There have also been bounteous spiritual rewards for him and his family. Since he took to heart the counsel that every member should be a missionary, Elder Kirby says his life has been filled with "unspeakable joy. It has brought a spiritual feeling into my life that I never dreamed would be possible."

He also encourages institute students to seek out those who are interested in learning of the Lord's ways. After President Russell Hulme of the San Jose West Stake challenged institute students "never to come alone to institute," Elder Kirby followed up by helping the students locate those interested in the gospel. At one institute event, students who brought non-Mormon companions got preference for the limited number of seats available.

"I have made it a personal objective never to allow a person to come into the institute building without my shaking his hand and personally welcoming him. This seems to develop an immediate rapport with young people and allows me to proceed into a gospel discussion," Elder Kirby said.

During registration at West Valley College's Saratoga campus, which adjoins the institute building and stake center, he has led institute students in passing out church tracts and copies of the Book of Mormon. More than 30,000 pieces of church literature have been handed out during three registration periods, resulting in several young people investigating and joining the Church.

Several times Elder Kirby, who is a stake missionary, and Clint McCready, the Latter-day Saint Student Association president, have visited Protestant and Catholic groups to explain the gospel.

"I have stressed to the students the importance of their being 'a light unto the world' and have told them that in every way they should be an example of the true followers of Christ. We have talked about proper dress, reverence, grooming, and language. I have also told them that they have no right to come to institute class and do anything, by way of questions or behavior, which would cause the Spirit to withdraw," Elder Kirby said.

Most of the student converts were friends of LDS students. Often Elder Kirby emphasizes to his students Joseph Smith's teaching that "friendship is one of the fundamental principles of 'Mormonism'; [it is designed] to revolutionize and civilize the world and cause wars and contentions to cease and men to become friends and brothers."

Everywhere he goes Dale Kirby is quick to offer a hearty handshake and a kind word, and, to those interested in listening, to explain the gospel. "I have made a commitment to ask at least one person the golden questions each day or to have at least one gospel discussion."

Church News, July 7, 1973, p. 11. Used by permission. In a two-year period since the publication of this article, more than ninety people have come into the Church through the efforts of Brother Kirby and his students.

"Do you know
the Church is true?"   *Sandy Steel*

I have a testimony that the Mormon Church is the true
church of Jesus Christ. A year ago I didn't know this, and I
was very unhappy and discouraged. I looked at the world,
saw all the things that were going wrong, and wanted to
know the reasons. I had dreams of making the world a better
place to live. I thought God must have forgotten the world,
and I was bitter toward him. Little did I know that he had
not forgotten me or the world, but he was going to lead me
step by step to the truth.

In high school, I had a very good friend, René Smith,
who was a Mormon. She was instrumental in my later taking
the opportunity to hear the gospel. A fine example, she lived
the gospel to the best of her ability. While I would continue
to look for my long-sought-after answers, she would lovingly
try to tell me that the answers were with God.

A friend of ours was going to be baptized one Saturday
afternoon, so René and I went to the service. It was there
that I first met Brother Kirby. When he found out I wasn't a
member of the Church, he came up to me and said, "I have
a strong feeling about you. Why aren't you baptized yet? Do
you know the Church is true? Can you tell me you know it
isn't?" I couldn't say that I knew it wasn't true, and I knew
that sometime in my life I was going to have to prove once
and for all that it wasn't true.

My next contact with Brother Kirby came as a surprise.
I had just finished registering for classes at school when I saw
him. He had a little table in the registration area with information on institute classes. He recognized me and we
talked a little, then he asked me some more of his questions
about why I wasn't looking for the truth in the Church. I decided I would sign up for an institute class, but I didn't really
think I would go. He asked if some friends of mine standing
nearby would be interested in some pamphlets. I said that I
didn't know, but he could try. He went over and gave each of
them a pamphlet. After he left, they all turned to me and

said, "Here, Sandy, we don't need these." I thought to myself, "You didn't even wait to see what it was about." Then I realized that I was just as bad as they were. I determined that I would go to the institute and find out about the gospel so I could have an honest answer to why I wasn't a member of the Church.

The first week I forgot about the class. The second week I remembered but was too scared to go in the direction of the institute. I decided the next week that I would go early and be there before a lot of people had come and I'd be scared off. I went over an hour early and Brother Kirby was very happy to see me. He took me into his office to talk. By the time class started, I had told him how I really felt, and I had agreed to take the discussions. I was wary and wondered if I was doing the right thing, but I was so happy that I already started to feel my burdens lighten.

I know that God was giving me strength and comfort after such a long time of being lost. From then on, it was a matter of taking the lessons and learning to pray and talk with God. I found the answers that I was looking for. I prayed about them, and the sweet, comforting Spirit filled me and witnessed to me that the Church is indeed true.

Report from a health missionary

Mary Ellen Edmonds

*W*hen I first received a call to serve as a health missionary, I knew very little about the program. I had a vision of myself headed into a deep, dark jungle, mounted on a carabao and ladened down with an eighteen-month supply of Band-Aids, aspirin, multicolored fly swatters, rubbing alcohol, shoelaces, insect repellent, snake-bite kits, bouillon cubes, and various first-aid manuals.

This vision has been shattered in the months I've been serving in the Philippines as a health missionary, but the one that has taken its place is so beautiful that I don't miss the carabao at all!

The health missionary program of the Church has been under way for two years now, but still many are asking, What is a health missionary? How do you get called to serve? What do you do?

Contrary to what many of us believe when we first hear of the program, we are not sent out to cure all the diseases on the face of the earth. We are not even called to treat the illnesses of the members of the Church, but rather to teach them principles of good health that will help them prevent disease. What a beautiful program!

We are called, as are other missionaries, to serve at our own expense for eighteen months or two years. Our calls come from the president of the Church, through our bishops. We go to the Missionary Home in Salt Lake City to spend time in language learning and/or our health program orientation. And then we're off to the Lamanites in the Dakotas, or south of the border to Uruguay, or all the way to the Philippines.

The Philippines is a marvelous country. There are many varieties of beautiful plants, trees, flowers, and fruits. Forty million of the most friendly, humble, wonderful people in the world live in this country of 7,100 islands. They speak 87 different dialects. They are remarkably gifted, particularly in music and handwork.

111

This is also a developing country and a land of many health problems. Manila is a crowded city with many people living in poverty. Thousands of families live on a salary of 50 pesos per month (about eight dollars) or less. There are typhoons and floods and flies and garbage. Pneumonia and tuberculosis are serious health problems.

Where and how do we begin to change this trend in the lives of our Church members and have some impact on their basic health? We have the advantage of a perfect organization already established and the direction of the priesthood. What a perfect way to reach the family and the individual— through the Church program, which is already functioning all over the world! We work with and train leaders who then share with the members. Under the direction of the district and branch leaders and our mission president, we help to gather resource material, determine health problems in specific areas, and formulate lessons and activities that can be adapted to various teaching situations. Because of the way our program works and the emphasis on health care rather than sick care, we can establish something that will endure long after we've gone home.

I have found that active members of the Church are generally in better health than their countrymen. I attribute this to their keeping the commandments, including the Word of Wisdom, and the purposeful living that comes with activity in the Church. These members already understand that their bodies are temples and must be kept clean and healthy. One humble sister, who has lost her husband and must work to have enough for her and her children, said to me with tears in her eyes, "Sister, I don't have enough money to buy what I know my children should eat, but I always express thanks to my Heavenly Father for the food I do have and ask him to bless it that it will give us health. And that makes all the difference."

We have opportunities to proselyte along with our work in the health program. There are probably few experiences in life that bring the same quality of joy as that of bearing witness to a family that God lives and that Jesus Christ is the

Savior of the world. Even if it is in a humble, two-room home, with mice running around on the floor, the rain coming in on our backs, one light globe to light the room, and a big mother pig bursting in in the middle of our testimonies, it still can be one of the most beautiful experiences life has to offer. We've had discussions with many interesting and interested people and have placed tracts and copies of the Book of Mormon in such places as the Department of Health, the World Health Organization, the Nutrition Foundation of the Philippines, and with taxi drivers, people on the bus, people at the post office, and even with Sister Ester, a delightful Catholic nun I met on a plane between Manila and Cebu. It was thrilling to see Sister Ester reading Alma.

One of the best things about a health mission is the association with the tremendous young people who serve on regular missions. Part of our work as health missionaries is concerned with keeping them healthy. We start with simple things like "boil your water and wash your hands." Then, somehow, we get the flu, and an elder asks innocently, "Did you forget to boil your water, Sister Edmonds?" We give the missionaries injections of the "gamma goblins" (gamma globulin), and many have laughed about "finally getting the point of the program." Sometimes we'll be engrossed in a book on the nutritional value of rice, and a missionary will ask humbly, "Are you sure that's one of the standard works?"

Words in hymns begin to have different meanings when we're singing them as health missionaries—"Thou flowing water, pure and clear," "With healing in thy wings," "With sleep refresh my feeble frame," "In every condition, in sickness, in health, in poverty's vale or abounding in wealth," "Feed us with knowledge and daily bread."

Scriptures, too, take on a new meaning. "And ye shall serve the Lord your God, and he shall bless thy bread, and thy water; and I will take sickness away from the midst of thee" (Exodus 23:25); "Thou shalt not eat any abominable thing" (Deuteronomy 14:3); "I have . . . drunk strange waters . . ." (2 Kings 19:24); "And there were some who died with fevers, which at some seasons of the year were very frequent in the land—but not so much so with fevers, because of the excellent qualities of the many plants and roots which God had prepared to remove the cause of diseases, to which men were subject by the nature of the climate" (Alma 46:40).

You grow a lot on a mission. Your feet grow flat, your leather books grow mold, your clothes grow thin, and your heart grows bigger. You learn a lot of things you didn't know before, like how to live without milk. You learn to make exotic noises with wet Hush Puppies as you walk down the street. You become better acquainted with Nephites, Israelites, and parasites. And through it all—the study sessions by candlelight, the rain on your bed in the middle of the night—you're thankful to be there and thrilled at all the things you have to write home about as you try to put into words the best two years of your life.

What or who is a health missionary, then? Someone who's going to learn and share a lot for a few short months, someone who will gain much more than he or she will ever be able to give. A health missionary is not necessarily a nurse or doctor. It is possible for Church members with many different skills to participate in this great, beautiful, and inspired program. The potential is exciting.

This is a labor of love and an opportunity to represent the Savior. And he is our greatest example, for truly he was ever concerned with both the physical and spiritual health of all he met.

New Era, June 1973, p. 52. Used by permission of the author.

"I'm that dirty little Irish kid"

Charles A. Callis

I remember the story that Brother Charles A. Callis used to tell us. There was a missionary who went over to Ireland and had filled a mission of two or three years. They invited him to the stand to give his homecoming speech, and he said to them something like this: "Brothers and sisters, I think my mission has been a failure. I have labored all my days as a missionary here and I have only baptized one dirty little Irish kid. That is all I baptized."

Years later this man came back and went up to his home somewhere in Montana. Brother Callis, now a member of the Council of the Twelve, learned where he was living and went to visit him. He said, "Do you remember having served as a missionary over in Ireland? And do you remember having said that you thought your mission was a failure because you only baptized one dirty little Irish kid?"

"Yes."

"I would like to shake hands with you. My name is Charles A. Callis, of the Council of the Twelve of The Church of Jesus Christ of Latter-day Saints. I am that dirty little Irish kid whom you baptized on your mission."

Harold B. Lee, *Speeches of the Year,* Brigham Young University, November 9, 1954, p. 1.

"Be still, and I will save you"

C. V. Spencer

The priests were for some time banded together in a secret organization. They soon became, however, more bold, and during a visiting tour among the branches of my district I was warned while walking in the road that something was wrong in Norwich, England. I went immediately to that place, and before I reached my room I was met by two brethren, who said, "There is a big anti-Mormon meeting at St. Andrew's hall."

I replied, "Very well, I will brush up and go to it." They and others whom I met pled with me not to go.

When I entered the hall, I found it too densely packed for me to get a seat in the body of the house. On looking to the stand I counted seventeen of the prominent ministers of Norfolk and Suffolk comfortably seated. I said to myself, "I also am a minister and that is my place." I walked up and took a seat. There were two thousand people present at that meeting. At that time St. Andrew's hall ranked as the third finest hall in England.

The meeting commenced about 2:30 P.M., and it was about five o'clock when I entered. At half-past eight the chairman announced that if any member of the unfortunate Mormon Church was present, who had the hardihood and moral courage to attempt a defense after such an overwhelming exposure of their system as had been made that day to the citizens of Norwich, he would be allowed to speak. Of course, all eyes had been on me and the invitation was a trap on the part of the ministers. They offered me no way of getting to the pulpit, as I was behind five rows of seats, each of which was packed with my opponents, and not one offered to allow me to pass. I prayed, put my hands on the sides of the heads of the two ministers in front of me, made an opening, and stepped over into their seat; this I did with the others until I reached the pulpit.

A great part of what I said I did not know at the time, nor have I known since, but near the close of my remarks I found myself with my back to the congregation and my face to the preachers. My last words to the latter were, "You are infidels, and it is you who make infidels, and by your precepts smother the hope of any realization of the gifts and blessings promised by Christ and his apostles. I prophesy, moreover, to you in the name of the Lord Jesus Christ, that your labors of this day and night shall be the cause of hundreds embracing the gospel I preach."

After I ceased to speak, the chairman undertook to read from the Book of Mormon, but he shook so that it was impossible for him to read. Another man tried to speak, but he was affected in the same way and had to desist.

There was a stairway leading from where I stood down to the vestibule, and I hoped to reach it soon enough after the dismissal to make my escape; but when I got there it was full of human beings, who were, however, more like devils than men. They shouted, "Where is he? Tear him limb from limb. Throw him over into the river," etc.

A tall man wearing a cloak could see me while the rest seemed blinded. He came up, covered me entirely with his cloak, slipped his arms under mine, drew me up to his bosom, and whispered, "Be still, and I will save you." He carried me out of the vestibule, the courtyard, and nearly a block up the street, the mob crowding up against and around us the whole distance. My deliverer worked his way to the side of the street until he got to his own home, where he struck the spring of the door in the stone wall. It flew open, and he cast me in like a log of wood and then passed on with the crowd. In about three-quarters of an hour he came back with some of our people, and I was liberated and guarded on the way home. The next day I presented this man with the best bond set of our publications I could procure. I asked him why he saved my life, to which he replied that it was only because of the love of justice.

From the time of this occurrence the work prospered as it had never done before. Our chapel was literally packed, and some citizens even took out every window on one side, brought their own trussel and planks, and built a platform the entire length of the building. On one occasion we went out after the evening meeting and baptized seventeen persons, and the conversions during the whole time were quite numerous.

Laborers in the Vineyard, Salt Lake City: Juvenile Instructor Office, 1884, p. 23.

"Lost" scripture leads to conversion
June Krambule

Colonel Robert E. Wilson, Ft. Bragg, North Carolina, remembers that dreary, depressing day in Vietnam and the "lost" scripture that led to his conversion.

It was August 15, 1969. As commander of an infantry battalion, he had called a memorial service for a young specialist who liked to be called "Squeak."

Squeak's tragic death the day before weighed heavily upon Colonel Wilson, not only as a grievous casualty of war, but also as a great personal loss. He thought of the pact Squeak had made with him, promising, "If you'll take care of the thousand men assigned to you, I'll personally watch out for you."

One day Squeak had driven away from the command in a jeep. Suddenly there was a deafening explosion of a mine and a rising cloud of smoke. The battalion commander, then a lieutenant colonel, was the first to reach the scene of the burning jeep. After a frantic attempt to reach Squeak, Colonel Wilson found only scattered fragments of a body.

Now, as the time for the memorial service approached, darkness closed in with a downpour of rain that shut out all rays from the sun. It would be impossible for a helicopter to bring in a chaplain.

Colonel Wilson wondered if he could possibly conduct the service, which must soon start. "I was feeling so depressed I knew I would have trouble running a service," he recalled. "It was at this point that a good Lord provided for our needs. A young captain, who was the artillery battery commander on my firebase, stepped up to me and said he was an ordained priest in his church. The young man did not mention the name of the church."

Colonel Wilson remembers this service as "very inspirational." He said, "The young man closed the service with a verse of scripture that just struck out and hit all of us very hard."

It read, "And behold, I tell you these things that ye may learn wisdom; that ye may learn that when ye are in the service of your fellow beings ye are only in the service of your God."

After these touching words, Colonel Wilson, grateful and moved, asked where he could find this scripture. The young man answered: Mosiah, chapter 2, verse 17.

"Well, I looked through my Bible, and I looked and looked," explained Colonel Wilson, "but I just could not find any book of Mosiah."

The following day he asked again, and, in fact, wrote the information down after carefully checking the spelling.

"Two days later I called the captain in and challenged him to find and show me the book of Mosiah in my Bible. He came armed with his serviceman's Book of Mormon," said Colonel Wilson. The young captain then gave the book to the colonel, and it is a prized possession today.

"I read the Book of Mormon once and did not understand all of it," Colonel Wilson said. "But when I read it again, I began to find peace of mind and acquired strength from some of the verses."

When he returned to his family at Ft. Bragg and resumed regular reading of scriptures in the evening, Colonel Wilson began reading favorite passages from the Book of Mormon.

A sort of family home evening developed, said petite, pretty Sister Wilson, although at that time the family knew nothing about the Church beyond the scriptures contained in the book.

Later they became friends with an LDS chaplain who arranged to have missionaries visit them when they became settled in Alexandria, Virginia, upon the colonel's assignment to the Pentagon.

On May 15, 1971, Colonel and Sister Wilson, along with two of their children, were baptized into the Church in the Mt. Vernon Ward, Annandale Virginia Stake.

Church News, August 30, 1975, p. 10. Used by permission.

A folded piece of paper

Nicholas G. Smith

Nicholas G. Smith had been home from his mission to Holland for some time and was comfortably located in Farmington, Davis County, with his wife, Florence Gay (whom he had married in 1906), and their three children. Then he was called to Salt Lake City by the president of the Church, who said to him, "My brother, we think it is about time one of your father's sons was in the mission field. How do you feel about it?"

Elder Smith replied, "Whatever you think about my father's sons, they will do."

"Well," said the president, "we would like to have you go down to South Africa."

In fifteen days Elder Smith and his family were on their way to the mission field in spite of the fact that their baby was sick. Upon arriving at Montreal, Canada, he received a letter from one of the apostles containing this statement: "The winds and the waves will be controlled in your interests." Elder Smith testified that they witnessed a literal fulfillment of that promise. During the winter months in the North Atlantic the waves usually roll high, but on the entire trip not a "white cap" was seen; the ocean was almost as smooth as glass.

Shortly after the arrival of the Smith family at the mission headquarters, the government of South Africa refused to let any more missionaries land in that country. Two elders came to the mission field about three weeks later and were deported, and soon thereafter five others arrived and they also were sent out of the country. Another elder, Franklin D. Price, decided that instead of going down the west coast of Africa and landing at Capetown, he would take a boat through the Mediterranean, through the Red Sea and along the east coast of Africa to Lourenso Marques, and thence by train to Capetown. This round-about trip used up all of his money, making it necessary for him to telegraph to the mission office for some to be sent to Lourenso Marques.

He must have twenty pounds to permit him to enter the country. When the ship docked at the port, as Elder Price was walking down the gangplank, he saw a folded piece of paper lying at the foot of the runway. He picked it up, put it in his vest pocket, and went to the telegraph office. He was discouraged when he found there was no money for him, but he decided he would get on the train and take his chances.

As the train approached the South African frontier, immigration officers came through the train questioning the passengers, and coming to the elder, they asked him about his money. Instinctively his fingers went into his vest pocket as he was wondering what reply to make. He felt the piece of paper and pulled it out; then, unfolding it, to his surprise he discovered it to be an endorsed check, with the government revenue stamp on it, for nineteen pounds and some shillings. The agent of the government took it, turned it over, and handed it back, saying, "That is all right." And he was permitted to enter.

An hour later, when he was met by President Smith and others at the depot, Elder Price wept as he unfolded his story. He felt that the Lord had indeed opened the way for him to get to his field of labor.

Thomas C. Romney, *The Gospel in Action* (Salt Lake City: Deseret Sunday School Union Board, 1949), p. 219.

A missionary's mother

Petra G. de Hernandez

I am a mother whom the Lord has blessed with four children, Floralba, Rosa Elida, Juan Sergio, and Delia Palmira. Nineteen years ago my husband died in an automobile accident. It was then that I felt the need to find God, so that he could help me with my family. My youngest daughter was eleven months old.

One night, in the midst of my desperation and finding myself alone with my children, I prayed to the Lord as if I were talking to another person. I asked him to show me the path to take in life. I told him that I knew he existed, but I didn't know where. I asked him to show me how or where to find him. I did it with such faith and desire to find the truth that I shall never forget that prayer.

The answer to my prayer was not long in coming. One morning two young missionaries knocked on my door and said they were from the Mormon Church and that they brought me a very important message. I had heard about the Mormons, but I had not been the least interested in them. I let them come in and they began the first lesson. As I received the first lesson, I felt that what they were saying was true. After the second lesson I could feel that all they were telling me was true, and I told them I wanted to be baptized with my family. They told me that we could be baptized after the last lesson; and so it was. We were baptized in the Roma Ward in the city of Monterrey, Mexico. At the present time we belong to the Monterrey Stake.

Since the day we accepted the gospel our lives have changed completely. I was now sure that God hears our prayers. I was immediately called to work as the second counselor in the mission Primary and then as the president of this organization. At that time my eldest daughter, Floralba, was the only one who worked, and with great effort we were able to go to the Arizona Temple to be sealed. Later she moved to the United States, and then because of the same job she moved to England.

A short time after she arrived in England, she received a call from her bishop to fill a full-time mission. She knew we needed her, and she wrote to me asking my opinion. As I read her letter only one scripture came to my mind, the one in 1 Nephi 3:7 that says that the Lord never gives any commandment to his children without first preparing the way for them to obey it. When I finished reading her letter, I immediately answered, telling her to say to the bishop that she was ready to go on a mission and for her not to worry. The Lord would know what to do with us.

She was sent to the Andes Mission, which at that time included the countries of Peru, Chile, and Ecuador. While she was in Lima, Peru, the great earthquake took place that shook that city and left much death and destruction; but absolutely nothing happened to her or her companion even though they were riding along in a taxi at the time it hit and they could see the terrified people on the streets, crying and shouting. It was a great experience for her to see how the Lord protects those who serve him.

During the entire time of her mission she served with all her heart, soul, mind, and strength. Upon completing her mission, she returned to the United States and the Lord blessed her with a good companion whom she married in the Oakland Temple.

During the time Floralba was on her mission, the Lord blessed us with all that we needed, and we never lacked for anything.

Later my son, Juan Sergio, was called to serve a full-time mission. It was a great challenge to him, because he only lacked two years to finish his schooling in administrative mechanical engineering, and the call from the Church to serve was exactly two years. I reminded him not to forget that he was a bearer of the Melchizedek Priesthood and that he had made covenants with the Lord in the temple, as a year before he had received his endowment in the Arizona Temple. Now the Lord was calling him to be his representative for two years. My son thought about it, prayed, and accepted the call to be a missionary despite the criticism of friends and schoolmates. He was sent to the Mexico West Mission. During his mission my son grew in knowledge and testimony. He had the opportunity of being the branch president of two branches, and above all of taking the gospel to those who had not yet received it. Upon his return from the mission field, he was called to be the stake financial clerk; then he was ordained a seventy; next he was set apart as clerk of the Monterrey Stake and also was ordained a high priest while he was yet single. He knows that it is a great responsibility to be a high priest while he is still single. With the experience and strengthening of his testimony that he got in the mission field, and with the inspiration of the Lord, he knows that he can continue fulfilling the wishes of the Lord. Next year he will finish his university studies and continue preparing himself for anything the Lord may assign to him in the future.

Six months after my son returned home from the mission field, my daughter Rosa Elida was called to fill a full-time mission. She asked for a two-year leave from her job in a government office, but then decided to quit so she could fill her mission, thereby losing all the rights she had acquired after eight years of working there. She was sent to the Mexico West Mission.

In all these years I have watched how the Lord has blessed us and blesses those who serve him. I have been able to experience the scripture, ". . . seek ye first the kingdom of God, and his righteousness; and all these things shall be added unto you." (Matthew 6:33.) Only my daughter Palmira is left to go on a mission, and this in accordance with whether the Lord calls her and according to her own desires. At the present time she is a teacher. I know that she has a testimony of the gospel. I can say with assurance that we are a united family due to the gospel and to those two missionaries who knocked on my door fifteen years ago.

I will always be grateful to them both for having knocked on my door, and I know there are people who are grateful that my children have been the missionaries who knocked on their doors to bring them the gospel. Last year at the Oakland Temple in California, I had the opportunity to meet again the missionary who baptized me. There is truly an indescribable joy in meeting those who brought you the gospel.

The Lord said that in serving others we are serving him, and one way to serve others is through missionary work. It is a privilege and a blessing for a mother in Zion to have a child in the mission field, because she is helping the Lord in his work. One of the duties of fathers and mothers as members of the Church is to support and sustain missionary work and see that their children go on missions. Perhaps it will mean sacrificing so that their children can go, but don't forget that some parents sacrificed so their children might knock on doors and that one of those doors was yours or your ancestors'. I know by personal experience it is necessary that we sacrifice a little so our children can go on missions. But I also know by personal experience that sacrifice brings blessings, because the Lord fulfills his word in his due time.

I know the Church is true and that it is directed by Jesus Christ. I can say with certainty that if we seek first the kingdom of God and his righteousness, all else will be added unto us at the proper time. I say it because I have experienced the reality of it. I have trusted in what the Lord has said through his servants, the prophets, and he has come through for me and my family, and I know the Lord will come through for those who trust in him and his servants.

This is my humble testimony, a testimony that cannot be purchased for any price in the world. I know the day will come when I will be before the Lord and will have to give him an accounting of my life and what I did with my family, and I hope to be able to say, "Lord, I have done my work."

International Magazine, published by The Church of Jesus Christ of Latter-day Saints, December 1975, p. 24. Used by permission.

*D*uring the years that William Moroni Palmer served on his second mission as the president, he experienced considerable hardship due to lack of financial aid. In the fall of 1881 he was to hold a conference with the Saints in Minnesota, but at the time all of his personal effects had been burned in a fire that destroyed the home of one of the Saints. He had no money and but one suit of clothes, and it was patched. Two weeks before the conference was to be held, greatly to his surprise, he received ten dollars from a little girl in Logan, Utah, whom he had never met but who had heard of his misfortune. She had collected the money from her little playmates. A few days later he received a contribution of twenty-five dollars from the Sunday School in Logan whose members had heard of his financial straits; and these contributions, together with seven dollars received from home, enabled him to purchase a suit of clothes for conference.

At the conference there was a rich outpouring of the Spirit of the Lord, and the gift of tongues was evident. Many Scandinavian Saints present, who could not speak or understand English, testified they clearly comprehended the sermon of Elder Palmer.

Upon another occasion, as he got off the train at Pontiac, Michigan, he found he had only one dollar. It was dusk, and the air had a tang about it that made him feel uncomfortable. He approached a policeman and asked if he could tell him where he could get a cheap but respectable place for the night. He was informed where he could get supper, bed, and breakfast for one dollar. As he was passing an alley, a little boy came running out, half-clothed, and asked if Elder Palmer would please give him ten cents with which to get something for his little sister to eat. She was crying for food and the mother was ill.

The heart of the elder was touched and he handed his only dollar to the child and said, "Take it to your mother and God bless you." Then the little boy disappeared and Elder Palmer made his way to the business section of the city.

Passing an open door to a doctor's office, the missionary stepped inside; and as he did so, the physician said, "What can I do for you, stranger?" The reply was, "I saw a fire here and I thought I could get warm." "Certainly," said the doctor and gave him a chair. Brother Palmer then explained who he was and the nature of his mission, which brought forth the statement from the doctor, "Is it possible that you are so far from home without money? If so, come home with me and you can stay as long as you like at my home." The doctor had a lovely home, and a hearty welcome was given the missionary by the wife of the doctor, who stated that she had once heard a Mormon elder speak and was much impressed with his sermon.

The next morning Elder Palmer went in search of the home of the young boy to whom he had given the dollar the night before. He found the miserable hovel in which the family lived, and in answer to his knock on the door, the same boy opened it and immediately called to his mother, "This is the man who gave me the dollar last night." The mother responded, "The Lord must have sent you here. Come here; I want to shake hands with you. You don't know how much good that dollar did us last night. The little boy bought a little coal, some bread and butter, and made me some tea, and you don't know how much good that did me."

Opportunity was thus afforded the Mormon elder for explaining the gospel to the woman, and especially that portion relating to prayer and the healing of the sick through the anointing with oil. At her request, Elder Palmer took from his pocket a bottle of consecrated oil and administered to the sick woman. As soon as he removed his hands from her head, she exultantly exclaimed, "Oh, I am well! I am well! That pain has left my head, and I can get up now."

Elder Palmer returned to the home of Dr. Gray and reported the condition of the family he had just visited, and at once Mrs. Gray sent a nurse to look after the woman.

Then she sent a load of coal and she herself went to the store and purchased provisions for the family.

A meetinghouse was arranged for by the doctor, and the elder held a meeting the following evening with the result that Mrs. Gray and the woman who was healed by Brother Palmer ultimately joined the Church, as did others in that community.

Thomas C. Romney, *The Gospel in Action* (Salt Lake City: Deseret Sunday School Union Board, 1949), p. 153.

The good man award

*Stephen C. Johnson**

We have three Eagle Scouts in our family—my brother and I and my dad. Three of Dad's brothers are Eagle Scouts, and we have many relatives and friends who have attained that rank in Scouting. So I do not want you to think that I do not appreciate the honors due to Eagle Scouts, because I do.

But in our family we have a homemade badge that is every bit as important to us as the Eagle badge. The star at the top of our badge is a Cub Scout service star minus the yellow circle. That is what fastens it to the shirt when it is presented. The blue and red ribbon was part of something Dad won a long time ago, and that ribbon is hooked to the metal pendant by a piece of copper wire. Carefully lettered in red enamel, the words "Good Man" shine forth on the silver shield.

I guess the medal was my idea, and Dad helped me make the medal before Bob left on his mission to Canada. At our last family meeting before Bob's departure, we gathered around and presented the medal to Bob. Somehow, on that occasion, we realized that the Good Man award represented something higher and more important than any other awards Bob had earned.

Bob had received his Eagle from Judge Gregg at a public ceremony we will never forget. It recognized his attainment of excellence as a boy, as did his earning the Duty to God award. Then why would this homely, handmade caricature of a medal, unauthorized by any organization whatsoever except his parents, brothers, and sisters, and presented to Bob as a complete surprise, have any special meaning to him?

I guess badges and medals are only outward symbols of what should exist within a person. The meeting of special goals is good, the recognition of such is proper, and the progress measured thereby is desirable.

---

*As told to Robert F. Johnson.

Some boys and men accomplish things for medals, for money, for praise, and for various other reason. But the truly great ones achieve for no such reasons but rather because they love the children of God and seek to help them.

Perhaps that is why the Good Man award represented something higher than the Eagle Award. It was presented as a token of love, understanding, and respect by his family who knew him intimately, faults and all. It was an indication of our faith in his mature character, his citizenship in the kingdom of God on earth, and his physical, mental, moral, and spiritual fitness to carry out the purposes for which he was born into our family.

I forgot about the small creation of cloth, paint, and metal, although Mom had carefully tucked it away. During the last family home evening before I was to leave on my mission to England, the Good Man award was again activated, to my surprise, and was pinned on me with the same gesture of love and respect with which it had been given to Bob.

I think, now I am on my mission, that Mom has once again tucked the Good Man award away in a drawer for the time when my younger brother, Eric, now a first class Scout, will prove himself worthy of it, as I fully expect he will. And I am not at all sure but what my sisters will wear it proudly at intimate family gatherings when they achieve similar milestones in life, for without them and their refining influences, where would we men be? My sweet mother, thrice a den mother and once an acting father while Dad was off to war, serving as an army medic, has earned the Good Man award over and over.

Truly, being a Good Man is greater than any award that could be given to our family. It is greater than anything made by human hands or created by human thoughts. It is achieving the potential given to us by our God, our Creator, and our Father in heaven.

The Eagle Scouts in our family have all used that award

to unlock the door to their own potentials. That is why each has truly become a Good Man.

New Era, October 1972, p. 18. Used by permission of the authors.

Byung Sik Hong of Seoul, Korea, attended his first Church meeting at a U.S. military base where several hundred uniformed Mormons nearly wrung his hand off in their characteristic welcome of a native investigator. After his baptism, Hong sought every opportunity to tell his countrymen of his newfound faith. When he ran unsuccessfully for office in the Korean parliament, he even listed on his campaign posters "I am an elder of The Church of Jesus Christ of Latter-day Saints" as one of his qualifications as a candidate.

Upon completion of his studies at Seoul University, he was conscripted into the military, as was common at the time. As a result of a confrontation with a superior officer over a matter that he felt involved his conscience, Hong was confined several weeks in a military jail. He soon discovered that his cellmates viewed religion and the religious with great disdain. With considerable courage, he announced that he was both a Christian and a Mormon.

The cell in which Hong and his fellow military prisoners were held had been furnished, by a Christian Missionary Society, with a copy of the Holy Bible. Several of the prisoners tore pages from the Bible, rolled tobacco in them, stuck them into the corners of their mouths, lit them, and said, as they blew their smoke in Hong's face, "So you're a Mormon, are you? Well, let's talk about your religion."

So Hong talked about his religion. For days, the gospel of Jesus Christ occupied the hours of confinement in that spartan cell. The remaining pages of the Bible were flipped back and forth and passed from hand to hand as Hong explained his convictions. What a curious thing it was, a few weeks later, for two tall American missionaries to stoop their way into this same cell to interview several prisoners who had expressed the desire to be baptized. The interviews

---

*This story was told to Lloyd N. Andersen in Ogden, Utah, when Byung Sik Hong visited the USA and received his endowments in the Salt Lake Temple.

revealed that they were completely worthy for baptism. And even more curious was the scene a few days later when, with the permission of the military authorities, the missionaries took their "prisoners" down to the ocean under guard and baptized them.

"He has not enough sense to be frightened"

William McBride

*A*t a conference in the fall of 1863, while on my Sandwich Island mission, a question came up relative to publishing the Book of Mormon in the Hawaiian language. Whether to have 5,000 copies printed, or to purchase a press, type, paper and ink and do the work ourselves—as we had printers of our own—was the subject of discussion.

It was decided that we would purchase the materials and print the book ourselves. The money was raised by subscription and loan, and I was appointed to go to San Francisco and make the purchase.

My trunk was packed and put on board the brig *DeJoniral,* but I had not a single dollar in my pocket to pay my passage. I told the brethren to exercise all the faith they could, while I called on Cody and Co., ship agents of the line, and asked them to take my note of hand, payable in San Francisco, and give me a certificate, which they did, although they were no friends of ours.

I presented the certificate, which called for first class fare, to Captain Jones, who told me that the berths were all taken, but he would give me the lounge in the after cabin to sleep on. All moved quietly for about eight days, when, having recovered from seasickness, I began to form acquaintances with the passengers and became known as a Mormon.

An agent of the whaling fleet by the name of Perkins, with his two servants, was on board, and he objected to my using the lounge. My bed was then placed in the steerage on sacks of grain.

The first night after my bed was moved, a heavy storm arose and drove us off our course to the north. The weather turned very cold, raining, hailing, and blowing a hurricane.

After the storm slacked a little, I came out of the hatchway and sat on the side, holding on while the ship tumbled from side to side amid the waves.

Mr. Perkins called out, "Look at that _____ Mormon; he has not sense enough to be frightened."

Then the first mate came, and after seating himself beside me, said, "Mr. McBride, did you not enter for San Francisco? What would you think if we should land you among the rocks of Oregon?"

I replied, "It makes but little difference with me, only so I land among the human family—my mission is to all the world."

He left me sitting with an overcoat and blanket wrapped around me and went and conversed with his associates.

Soon after, the captain came beside me and told me that he intended to make one more voyage. At this time the storm had increased to a heavy gale, and the captain, throwing himself suddenly into his seat in the cabin, exclaimed, "I can do nothing more!"

I said to him, "We shall all go into San Francisco, and not a hair of our heads shall be lost; but we shall have to be helped in."

Soon the storm ceased and the sun shone, when it was ascertained that we were 400 miles north of our due course. Then all hands set to work, mending and setting the sails, and we soon got under way in a very rough sea, but all passing pleasantly.

I still remained in the steerage but otherwise enjoyed all the privileges of first-class passengers, until we came in sight of San Francisco, with a light breeze. At this point the indomitable Perkins imagined anchorage already secure, and exultingly said, "We are going in without help, and that Mormon has told one _____ lie."

Before we came to the mouth of the gate, however, a strong wind arose and drove us back. The captain signalled for a tug—we were drifting toward the rocks, but the tug hooked on just in time to save us.

We got in at dusk and all the passengers went on shore but myself. In the morning the captain took me to shore, called for an omnibus, and took his trunk and mine to his room in a hotel.

I went up into the city to Brother J. M. Horner's and raised my passage money, and Brother Chapman Duncan went to the hotel, lifted my note, and took my trunk and valise to Brother Horner's.

We made search and learned that we could not obtain a suitable printing press and fixtures in San Francisco, so I deposited the purchase money in the bank. I then made arrangements with Brother Horner and he sent a check to his agent in the east, and the press was soon forwarded.

Juvenile Instructor, vol. 16, p. 70.

"We sacrificed
our all"
Brent R. Esplin

*E*lder Lynn Bodily and I were assigned to reopen a new area in upstate New York. Upon our arrival we located a box of materials left by the previous missionaries. In the box was a list of past contacts for the area, and on that list was the name Lois Gilson. We phoned her, along with the remaining people on the list, and requested an appointment. In our discussion with her, she indicated that she had heard of the Church through a visit to the Hill Cumorah Pageant with a nonmember friend. She said she had studied the Church and felt it was true and that Joseph Smith was a prophet, but she didn't have enough strength to quit smoking.

We met with Sister Gilson for about eight weeks on a regular basis. Each time we would teach her the principles of the gospel and try to help her find the strength to live the Word of Wisdom. It became evident that she was increasing in her understanding but still lacked that inner conversion.

One day she told us she was going to New York City for a business convention. She said she would try to live the Word of Wisdom on this trip, and if she succeeded, she knew she would have enough strength to observe it in any situation.

On the day of her departure, we began a fast in her behalf. Upon her return we met with her and she told us of her experience. She sadly said it was too hard to quit smoking, that she "just couldn't make it." We returned home discouraged and disappointed.

The next morning we stopped by her home for a few minutes. She answered the door and immediately we could see a change in her. She was almost glowing. We didn't think much about it—it was probably just a happy day for her.

That evening we returned for a final visit. She still had that glow, so we inquired as to her reason for being so happy. She told us the following experience: "After you left Sunday, I prepared for bed and said my prayers as usual. Then I went to sleep. At midnight I woke up and lit up my usual cigarette. As I did so, I thought, 'Why should I feel guilty about smoking? I am not a Mormon.' At that moment my wall seemed to open, and coming into my room seemed to be a long procession of handcarts. As I watched, I realized they were Mormons. One couple came directly toward me and said, 'Sister Gilson, we walked 1,600 miles for this church and sacrificed our all, and you can't even live the Word of Wisdom!' At this point the experience ended and I made up my mind that I would never smoke again and that I must join the Church."

The feeling in the room was magnificent, to say the least. She then bore her testimony and we filled out her baptismal recommend. She is now a member of the Massena Branch in Massena, New York.

*A*fter bouncing down a dirt road in a packed bus for four hours, I finally arrived in Concepcion del Uruguay, Argentina, and was met by two other missionaries. I was to play a piano recital that night in the auditorium of the Colegio del Uruguay.

After checking the auditorium's piano and making sure everything was in order for the recital, we returned to the apartment for a short siesta.

That evening as we left for the concert, we heard noise and shouting down the street. One of my companions told me he had heard that an anti-Yankee demonstration was scheduled, stemming from the death of Chile's President Allende, which had occurred that very morning. The elder said we did not have to worry, because the demonstration was taking place in a plaza on the other side of town. We avoided the crowds by walking an extra block out of the way.

Soon after we arrived at the auditorium we heard a noise through the backstage window. A mob carrying torches, communist flags, and banners was coming toward the auditorium. We barely had time to bolt the back door to keep the mob out. Ten demonstrators managed to get in the half-filled auditorium before the management could lock all the doors. The other half of our audience was unable to enter.

We later learned that the mob had read in the newspapers that a U.S. pianist was presenting a concert. They had planned to drag the *yanqui* from the auditorium and make him—me—the climax of the demonstration.

Outside the auditorium's locked doors the mob began to shout and chant, *"Fuera yanqui, fuera yanqui!"* (Yankee go home!) and *"Hallar, hallar, en la lucha popular!"* (Become part of the common fight!) They strung up an effigy and set fire to it, and the demonstration continued for an hour and a half before the police could break it up.

The sponsor of the concert came backstage and asked

me if I wanted to go ahead and perform, even though half the audience was still outside.

At the end of the evening, after I had finished performing, three of the demonstrators who had come into the hall came up to talk to me and my companions. In our conversation I asked them why they had come.

"We seriously came to kill you," one answered. He then asked us who we were.

"We're Mormon missionaries."

"I've never heard of the Mormons before."

We asked him the golden questions. Later this eighteen-year-old youth invited us to his house to explain the gospel. A month later he was baptized. His family was converted also. The last I heard, our demonstrator-convert was preparing for a mission.

New Era, September 1975, p. 7. Used by permission of the author.

"If you are willing to pay the price"
Lynn Del Mar

David and Nellie had been married four years. Being isolated on a ranch twenty miles from friends, near the Canadian Rockies, had made them very close to each other. Fundamentally they had been happy, but there were moments in Nellie's life, particularly when she was alone, that were distressing. Something from within seemed to be protesting. Silently, but truthfully, she admitted dissatisfaction with some of her accomplishments.

David was not a member of the Church. Nellie had married him because of her love for him, believing implicitly that she could convert him. Since their marriage, he had gradually grown more indifferent. Any attempts on her part, or that of her friends, to discuss religion seemed to increase his determination to avoid the subject. Finally he informed his associates that they could be better friends if religion were left out of all their conversations.

About this time, Brother Marlene and his companion were assigned as home teachers to visit the home of David and Nellie. It was a forty-mile trip; and in the winter when the snow was deep, two days were required to make the visit.

The first visit was made during the winter, and by invitation the home teachers stayed overnight. David proved to be a splendid host until religion was mentioned, and then, as usual, he requested that it not be discussed.

Conforming to his wishes, they spent a pleasant evening, and when it was time to retire, Brother Marlene asked the privilege of kneeling in prayer with the couple. This was granted, and prayer was offered; the prayer was a supplication for the blessings of the Lord to be upon the household.

Before the teachers left the next day, David asked a few questions about the gospel, but Brother Marlene answered, "I desire to be your friend, so probably we should not discuss religion." David, however, invited them to visit regularly each month.

The next month a very pleasant evening was spent, but

unlike the first visit, the gospel was discussed until the early hours of the morning. As the teachers prepared to leave the next day, Nellie called Brother Marlene aside and said, "I would give anything if David could see the truth of the gospel and would join the Church."

"Nellie," he said, "I am going to take you at your word. I am prompted to make you a promise: if you are willing to pay the price, you will realize your desire." Then he said, "Do you keep the Word of Wisdom?"

Her eyes dropped. She said, "Well, you see, David does not understand. He likes tea and coffee, and to be friendly, I use them too, but I have told him about the Word of Wisdom."

"Yes," said Brother Marlene, "but how much influence do your words have when your life does not conform to the teachings you advocate?"

Another month passed, and as the home teachers approached, Nellie met them, saying, "How happy I am! David has discontinued using tea and coffee. When he observed that I was not using them, he said, 'Why aren't you drinking tea or coffee?' Then I replied, 'I have been unfair to you. I have been taught the Word of Wisdom from my youth, but I have not been strong enough to live it. I have told you of its value, and yet I have broken it myself, not realizing what a poor example I was setting.' The next morning when I was preparing breakfast, David said, 'Don't make tea or coffee for me anymore.' "

Before leaving the next morning, Brother Marlene said, "Nellie, do you pray?" She paused and then said, "No, I do not. David has never believed in prayer, and after we were married, we had so much company, I just forgot to pray."

"But you say you believe in prayer?"

"Yes, I do," she replied.

"How strong is your belief? Surely it is not faith, for faith moves one to action. You know your promise. Are you willing to keep it?"

"Oh, yes, I am," she answered.

"Then I think you should ask your husband to kneel in

143

prayer with you. If he objects, you continue your prayers faithfully, and he will join you."

The next month brought further progress, and as a pleasant evening was concluded, David said, "May we have a word of prayer before we retire?"

Before leaving, Nellie was asked, "Do you pay tithing?"

"No. You see, David does not believe in tithing, and he earns the money."

"But," said Brother Marlene, "don't you have an allowance? The Lord says we should tithe our income, and ten cents is tithing on one dollar and is as acceptable in the sight of the Lord as one hundred dollars is on one thousand dollars. If you believe the law of tithing, you should comply with it."

On the next visit, Nellie paid three dollars tithing. This was the first she had paid since leaving her home.

As the teachers concluded their visit the following month, David said, "I would like to pay some tithing, if you will accept it."

"Why do you pay tithing?" he was asked.

"Because my wife has proved to me the value of the blessings that will come to those who faithfully observe this principle."

Brother Marlene commended Nellie for the progress made in the conversion of David. "But," he said, "you have another very important step to make. You must get him to attend sacrament meeting."

"That will be difficult," she said. "He loves to go to the park each Sunday."

"You must impress upon him the necessity of properly observing the Sabbath day. This can only be done through your sincerity. Express a desire to attend church regularly, and urge him to accompany you."

David accepted Nellie's request, and as winter approached, they came regularly to sacrament meeting. Soon thereafter, he applied for baptism, and when the Alberta Temple was opened for ordinance work, he and Nellie were among those in the first company to receive their endowments and to be sealed in an eternal union.

When asked the question, "What influenced you most in your conversion?" David said, "I would rather see a sermon than hear one any day."

_____

Improvement Era, June 1947, p. 397.

"What was the man's name?"

Richard H. Cracroft

*I*t was time to end my mission. I had been released from the presidency of the Baden Branch in Switzerland, and I would spend my last week in the mission home in Basel.

I was anxious to begin my trip home, for though I had labored hard and filled a good mission—a memorable mission—I was looking forward with great anticipation to the joy of returning to my family. The Lord had blessed them greatly with prosperity, health, and strength. I was proud of how Mom had continued to bear the heavy burden she had assumed when Dad had suddenly gone blind in 1951. Dad had made a wonderful adjustment and, despite occasional periods of depression, had almost fully recovered his spirits. To the public, at least, he was the old Ralph Cracroft. But he soon became someone even greater, for in the face of an overwhelming handicap, he had shown a smiling face to the world, had rehabilitated himself, and had continued to serve the Church as well as before. I was proud of them both and anxious to see them again.

I was to be in the mission home that last week, doing odd jobs but also helping a newly arrived group of elders learn the lessons and become accustomed to their new assignments.

I remember only one of these young men now. That morning we had climbed the stairs to the top floor of the mission home, where I was to interview and teach him. In our hour together he confessed to me that he had not been enthusiastic at first about coming on a mission; in fact, he had initially turned down the call. He had seethed with inward turmoil, not knowing whether he had the strength to complete a mission, to leave his girl, to postpone his education for that long.

This had been for him a dark period, as it occasionally is with the young man who dreads to cut—yet wants to cut—the ties that bind him, knowing that nothing will ever be the same again, knowing that he will have to commit himself to

146

service for two or more years. And a mission is no sheltered workshop; it is a battlefront, and a few casualties must be expected. But the triumphs are glorious.

Knowing this, and having experienced it all myself, I sympathized. I asked him to tell me what had made him change his mind, for he was here with me in Basel, Switzerland, an ordained missionary.

"It was an odd experience," he recalled. Torn by this inner turmoil, with doubts as to his future, he had attended a sacrament meeting in a friend's ward a few months ago. It had been a routine meeting until a man rose to speak with a firm and vigorous voice, a man who had been afflicted as an adult with blindness. This man recalled how the Lord had blessed him with deeper vision into the truths of life; how his soul had really come to see; how, in the midst of his affliction, one that most people deem to be the greatest affliction, he could praise his God for the richest blessing that could come to man. The blind man recounted how he had served the Lord all his life and how the Lord was now blessing him beyond measure with numerous opportunities.

The new elder paused, visibly moved. This man, he continued, had inspired him, and he had asked himself, "If such a man, from whom the Lord has taken the most precious gift of sight, can praise God for his blessings and bear a testimony of God's goodness, who am I to hold back my feeble gifts from the work of the Lord?" At that instant he decided to accept the call he had once refused. He went home and called his bishop to tell him of his change of heart.

"What was the man's name?" I asked.

"I don't know," he replied.

"I do," I smiled, through misty eyes. "I do."

Ensign, May 1971, p. 5. Used by permission of the author.

Elder John K. Lemon   *Charles A. Callis*

*T*he chilly autumn day was fast descending to its close. Behind the Georgia hills the sun was slowly setting. Over the country town of Hazlehurst the lengthening shadows were falling.

Elder John K. Lemon, a young missionary, was traveling without purse or scrip. He was seeking food and a sleeping place for the night. But everyone to whom he had appealed gave him the "cold shoulder."

People met him at the doorway, and they said, "Be of good cheer. You can stay with our next neighbor. We don't keep the Mormons here."

Tired, hungry, and dejected, he came to a farmhouse on the edge of the town. Elder Lemon was very apprehensive lest he should be obliged to enter into the deepening gloom of the woods and spend the night with "Uncle Sam." This meant, as every missionary knows who has had this experience, that he would sleep under the open sky, with leaves and grass for his bed, for his pillow his stick grip. He was worried.

Prayerfully refreshing his sorely tried faith, he approached the farmhouse and timidly knocked on the door. Mr. Dyal, the head of the house, appeared. He was a prominent farmer, well respected by the townspeople. With a look of wonderment he surveyed the humble supplicant from head to foot, for Elder Lemon wore a Prince Albert coat, the style of coat worn by the missionaries in those days. The pockets were bulging with tracts. A derby hat topped off his conspicuous wearing apparel.

"I am a Mormon missionary," said the elder. "Will you please give me food and shelter for the night?"

There was a moment's hesitation before a response to this appeal came. To the elder, it was a tense moment. Finally Mr. Dyal said, "Come in, and we will take care of you."

When the hungry and grateful preacher had done full

justice to a substantial southern dinner, the good man of the house said to him, "You are the first Mormon elder I have met. Explain Mormonism to me."

Elder Lemon, a tiller of the soil before his mission, was little experienced in the ministry. Entirely incapable of philosophical reasoning, which often lacks the illumination of the Spirit, he proceeded, in a humble way, to deliver his message. Plainly and earnestly, he bore his testimony that the gospel was the power of God unto salvation.

The power behind that testimony carried it to the hearts of Mr. Dyal and his family. The Lord, true to his promise, did not suffer that the words of his humble servant would be void and of no effect; he prospered them so that they accomplished that which he pleased. The gospel seed fell into good ground and brought forth fruit.

And now let Kossuth Dyal, one of the sons now living in California and writing long after this remarkable episode occurred, relate the sequel to the story. His letter follows: "Dear Brother Callis:

"I am very grateful to you for sending Kenneth [his missionary son] to attend my mother's funeral. I was unable to make the trip but as a result of your thoughtfulness I was represented through Kenneth. I am indebted to you more than words can express.

"The Southern people are my people. I know them. I am of them. They are a simple folk, but a more loyal citizenry very few districts or countries have produced.

"As a family we can never repay the Church for the two weeks' labor Elder John K. Lemon performed in our community. From this small beginning, twelve of our family became members of the Church. (I am referring to my father's family only.) All of the ten children are parents of from two to eleven, and the majority of the children are Latter-day Saints. Three of father's sons have been honored with approximately ten years of missionary service in the Southern States. There is no way for me to know the number brought into the Church through the missionary labors of my brothers, Forest L. and John L. Dyal, but in my weak way and handicapped to a great extent, I baptized 105 people. The only reason I refer to this is to call your attention to the apparently endless chain set in operation through the presentation of Mormonism to one family. The thought never occurred to Elder Lemon that such a body of recruits could be assembled in thirty years. Elder Lemon went hungry in our community, but thirty years later the brief review above shows that hundreds have been fed the bread of life on account of the seed of truth he planted deeply in my father's heart. I wish it were possible to have every young man see, as I do, the far-reaching influence and probable results of one man's labors.

"I am happy in the knowledge that my father and mother have been able to leave this sphere of existence with a testimony of the truth.

"May God bless the missionaries of the South that they may find hundreds looking for the gospel as Elder Lemon found us.

"Your brother in the cause of truth,

Kossuth Dyal"

Improvement Era, vol. 47 (1944), p. 658.

To share
a mission

Loren L. Richards

As members of The Church of Jesus Christ of Latter-day Saints, we should follow the admonition of our Prophet—to be missionaries and share the gospel and its blessings wherever opportunity may afford.

The anxious desire to be engaged in the Lord's work can be seen on the faces of those entering the missionary home, and we know they have been taught well at home to forgo the pleasures of dates, parties, and dancing, that they might reap the joys of the future by helping someone to see the light of the gospel. Joys not shared with others become a passing fancy, while those we share live on forever. To share a mission with the family is a wonderful experience, and parents have testified that the Lord certainly blesses those at home as well as those in the mission field.

One lady missionary, just before receiving her release, told her story:

"Father had become inactive and drifted away from the Church, and Mother lost interest. When the bishop asked me to go on a mission, I was almost afraid to tell them. Father hadn't been to church for a long time; and when my testimonial was held, both Father and Mother were asked to sit on the stand. I had been to my friend's farewell, and her father and mother were asked to say a word. This bothered me for fear my parents would turn down the offer. But to my surprise, Father gave a talk; and with tears running down his cheeks I heard him say, 'Please forgive me for taking the Church for granted, and I promise, when my daughter comes home, we will be ready to go to the temple and be sealed and united as a family.' Today I received a letter and the joyous message, 'I was ordained an elder last Sunday, and Mother and I are waiting your return that we can make that long-awaited trip to the house of the Lord.' "

Yes, missions are shared by families. Here are some stories of those coming to the missionary home.

"Eight years ago," writes John from Wells, Nevada,

"my father gave me a heifer calf so I could start a cow herd of my own. Each year he donated another heifer calf to me for my herd. We called this the 'Missionary Herd.' Whenever one of my cows had a bull calf, I traded him to Father for a heifer calf. Each year I sold enough of the offspring and older cows from my herd to pay my tithing and put the balance in the bank for my mission and later for college. At present I have twelve cows in my herd. Feed and pasture were paid for by my working for my father during the summer months and before and after school time."

David's home is in Arizona. His plans for a mission started five years ago when he began delivering newspapers. The money earned was put in the bank for the time when he would go on a mission. David says: "My day started at 4:30 A.M. By 7:00 A.M. I was at seminary. This was my schedule for four years of high school. I also participated in three major sports. Because of devoted service, the newspaper awarded me a $1,000 scholarship to the college of my choice. When my mission call came, I had my clothes and books purchased and was all ready to go."

Rickey, who is only seven years old, talks a lot about when he grows up and goes on a mission. He has found a wonderful friend, a widow known as Aunt Adele (Sister Bird), who has offered him a challenge: "For every dollar you save for your mission, Rickey, I'll match it." Rickey mows lawns and does various other jobs. Together these two make regular trips to the bank where a savings account, "For My Mission," has been set up. Since these two have started this fund, grandpas and grandmas have been adding to the fund for birthdays and other occasions. Rickey's eyes are full of sparkles. Already his heart is set on the day "when I go on my mission." When that day comes he will have enough saved for it.

Instructor, March 1962, p. 86. Used by permission of the author.

Survival of the British Mission during World War II   Andre K. Anastasion, Sr.

In July 1937 President Heber J. Grant, who with other Church officials was attending the British Mission centennial conference in Rochdale, Lancashire, made a prophetic statement to the effect that "every missionary from Zion will be removed from the British Isles."

On September 3, 1939, Great Britain declared war against Nazi Germany. By a joint order of the British and United States governments, all U.S. nationals not directly involved in the war were to leave the British Isles. This affected all of our missionaries from the United States.

By the end of 1939 some 130 missionaries left the shores of England. For the first time in 102 years the British Mission was left without a single missionary from Zion, and the prophecy of President Grant was literally fulfilled within two and a half years.

My two counselors, James P. Hill and James R. Cunningham, and I were set apart by President Hugh B. Brown, the retiring mission president, prior to his departure, and were to assume charge of the British Mission. Our appointment was confirmed by a cable from the First Presidency. I devoted my full time to the mission.

World War II was soon upon us in all its fury. London, the main target, was bombed almost day and night, and destruction of property and life was tremendous. But we remained with the Saints, and the Lord blessed us.

Our mission problems were many indeed. We appealed to our sixty-eight branches for local missionaries, and by the end of the first year we had almost four hundred of them ranging in age from seventeen to seventy-five. They devoted an average of five hours a week to missionary labors in helping the branches and in preaching the gospel. We also had twelve British full-time missionaries. In twos they stayed about four weeks in each branch, preached gospel sermons each Sunday, and then moved on. Thus, we were able to cover all the branches of the mission.

But the need for full-time missionaries during the war years was great indeed. At one of the Scottish District conferences held in Glasgow, when the question of missionaries was raised at the final session, I noticed an elderly couple and their daughter sitting together to my right on the front row. The daughter was using sign language to tell her parents what was being said.

When the final session was over, this young lady, Isabella McDonald, approached me somewhat timidly and said, "President, my parents are willing for me to go on a mission, but we have no financial means."

"Sister McDonald," I replied, "please tell your parents that I am grateful for their response and your faith to be a missionary. The Lord will open the way for you to go. I will be back in London on Monday evening and will write you on Tuesday."

At my desk on Tuesday morning, I began to open the numerous letters awaiting my attention. As I proceeded to open one, I read: "Dear President: I would like to support a missionary for six months, and enclose my first monthly check." The letter came from a British army officer, a member of the Church stationed somewhere in France. I immediately sent a letter and the check to Sister McDonald, who, in time, fulfilled a fine mission.

Upon receipt of a traveling visa, I went to Ireland to visit the districts of the mission. The morning I reached Belfast, the city was still smoldering from a heavy enemy air raid. Whole streets of houses and stores lay in ruins. The population of the city was in a state of shock. I spent that week visiting all of our members.

On Sunday we held our annual district conference in Belfast. We met in the afternoon on the top floor of a labor hall. The small congregation of about forty-five people was more than ever united after such a frightening air raid. The burden and the need of full-time missionaries was again before us, and I rose to my feet. Looking to my right, I saw Sister Joan Taggart among the Saints.

"Sister Taggart, I feel to ask you to go on a mission. Do

you think you will be willing to give six months of your time in the service of the Lord?"

She stood up. "President, I will be willing to go, but I have no means to support myself. My mother is a widow, and my only brother is in the British Navy. His monthly pay is so small that both Mother and I have to work."

"Sister Taggart, I am grateful for your response. I am not worried about the money. I want to give you a promise that the Lord will open the way and you shall have the money needed for your mission."

"I will be willing to go."

Then I looked to my left. "Sister Bannatyne," I said, "I feel to ask you to go on a short mission. Would you be willing to help the Church in these war times?"

"I am willing to go, but as you know, president, all of us five girls at home and our brother have to work to support our widowed mother and ourselves."

"The Lord will bless you and help you, and the way will be opened."

As we sang the closing hymn, a question crept into my mind. Where would the money come from?

After the hymn ended and the closing prayer was said, a member of the Dublin Branch came up to me. "President, I'll be happy to take care of Sister Taggart for six months." As she was writing a check, there stood a brother by the table. "I'll take care of helping Sister Bannatyne fulfill her mission."

Our final session was held in another hall, and the congregation was much larger. At the conclusion an American army officer spoke to me. "President, it has been some time since I have enjoyed such an outpouring of the Spirit of the Lord. Would you give me an opportunity of supporting another missionary?" His support was gratefully accepted, and another missionary was called.

Entrusted with the financial responsibility of the British Mission, I was left a sum of about two hundred pounds sterling (then $800) as mission funds, with the parting advice to go very carefully with that money, because "you may not get any more." From the monthly reports coming in, the tithes and fast offerings were often less than the funds requested by some of the branches, and I was constantly concerned about how to meet our financial obligations. Letters sent to the branch presidencies to encóurage members to a more faithful observance of the laws of tithing and fast offerings had not helped us, and I was afraid that our mission reserve would not last long, although we economized in every way possible. I was reluctant to dictate a letter to the headquarters of the Church for financial assistance, bearing in mind the parting advice given me. And to close some branches was unthinkable.

"There must be another way," I thought, "a better way to solve our financial problems together." Then I remembered the counsel of the Lord: "Ask, and ye shall receive; knock, and it shall be opened unto you. . . ."

More and more I asked the Lord in prayer for wisdom. One day after fasting, I told my wife that I intended to fast the next day also, as I had much on my mind. She looked at me very concerned and said, "You had better eat tomorrow and fast the next day." I followed my wife's advice and then continued altogether for thirty-five days, fasting every other day. This I did in all humility, having no other reason than to seek the Lord's guidance on how to solve our mission's financial situation.

After concluding my days of fasting and communion, I related to my counselors that during those thirty-five days I had received no impression at all about money—nothing about tithing or fast offerings. The only impression that manifested itself and continued with me was about the sacrament, and I felt the assurance that in this sacred ordinance of the restored gospel lay the answer and solution to our financial problem.

Before our annual district conference, we held an early sacrament and testimony meeting, and again I felt the same impression and assurance. After the bread and water had been blessed and passed to each one of us, I reflected on what we had done in partaking of the sacrament. We had asked our Heavenly Father to bless the bread and water, and we in turn had entered into a covenant to take upon ourselves the name of his Son, to always remember him, and to keep the commandments that he had given us. Then I asked those present if we had intelligently and conscientiously realized the covenants we had made, or if we had partaken of the sacrament as a matter of procedure. We realized that the answer to this could only be found within the heart and mind of each personally. I reminded those present of the words of the scriptures that the sacrament would be a curse to those who would partake unworthily, and suggested that each time we partake of the sacrament we should silently, with bowed heads, examine our conduct and our hearts so that we might always be true to our covenants and sacred obligations and manifest an intelligent faith by our works and deeds before the Lord. Thus we might enjoy his blessings.

"None of us would wish to bear false witness. A willful or careless disregard in failing to return the Lord's ten percent, obeying the Word of Wisdom, or observing the spirit of the sabbath would, in my opinion, constitute a false witness on our part. One cannot partake of the sacrament and bear sacred witness to God to follow him and then disregard his instructions," I said.

Then I was led to make this promise: "Your tithes and offerings will be returned to you, multiplied a hundredfold, as your inheritance in Zion, when the Lord shall come again."

The impression gained from my appeal was such that some of our members for a time stopped partaking the sacrament. They understood. But before long it was our joy to learn that most of the members were again partaking of the sacrament. The branch presidents were advised not to question those who still refrained, but to show them love and kindness, and to visit them often. It was particularly stressed that those who were called to administer the sacrament should repeat the sacrament prayers in a clear voice and pronounce each word distinctly and reverently, for it was a matter of personal witness and covenant between every Latter-day Saint and the Lord.

The British Saints took the appeal to heart, and there was evidence of sustaining faith and effort on their part. The monthly reports coming in were most encouraging, and I was spared the necessity of writing for financial assistance from Church headquarters.

It was almost four and a half years before President Brown was able to return to England and resume the responsibility of the British Mission. By then we had seventy-eight branches and fourteen districts under the local priesthood leadership. Over 500 local missionaries had labored during the war years. In addition, 105 full-time British missionaries had rendered fine service. Some of them gave of their labor and means for six months, some for one year, many for two years, and one elder for three and a half years. Marvelous blessings and faith-promoting experiences were witnessed by missionaries and members.

The British Mission prospered and progressed during the war years. Our baptisms were almost on a par with the pre-war record. And finally, when the mission records were transferred to President Brown, there was a surplus of over $80,000 in the mission funds—a small token toward the building of the temple in the British Isles, then (in 1944) only a cherished hope. [Fourteen years later the temple was built in the County of Surrey; it was dedicated on September 7, 1958, by President David O. McKay.]

We asked the Lord for help and we received intelligence—the light of truth—on how to solve by obedience to his commandments many of our mission and individual problems, and how to survive in faith and limb the crucial years of the World War II.

Improvement Era, April 1969, p. 60. Used by permission of the author.

The ultimate commitment

Byron A. Rasmussen

I arrived in the Denmark Mission in November 1956. My first assignment was in the city of Aabenraa, with Elder Vaughn Rasmussen from Salt Lake City as my companion. We met with an investigator by the name of Holger Ravn for several weeks. Not knowing the language very well, I could not tell how he was receiving the gospel, but there was a good spirit in our meetings.

When Elder Rasmussen was assigned as district leader in Copenhagen, I received a new senior companion, Elder Cal Juel Andreasen from La Canada, California. After a few meetings, Mr. Ravn made a commitment to be baptized. I did not learn the story that follows until a couple more months passed and I was able to understand the language better.

After each meeting with Mr. Ravn, Elder Andreasen would fill me in on the discussion on the way home to our apartment. Since it was a long way home by bike, we talked a lot about Mr. Ravn. My companion told me that he had a testimony but was afraid of the persecution that would follow baptism. He had a good job, but he was afraid his employer would fire him because he didn't want any Mormons working for him.

Finally my companion committed Mr. Ravn to baptism, and we made arrangements for his baptism a week later. We had to travel from Aabenraa to Espjerg, where there was a baptismal font, and before we left to catch the bus, Mr. Ravn asked us to administer to him. After a long bus ride we arrived at Espjerg and went straight to the church, only to find it locked tight. After looking all over for the district leader with no success, we returned to Aabenraa without baptizing Mr. Ravn.

It was some time until Mr. Ravn would even talk to us, but finally, with patience, long-suffering, and love unfeigned, we were able to recommit him to baptism. When the arrangements were made this time, there was no possible way they could go awry. We had the district president and branch president follow up.

When we arrived, all was in readiness and a beautiful service was held. As I walked down into the waters of baptism with Mr. Ravn, he gripped my hand tightly and his breath was coming in short gasps. I turned him around and assumed the proper position, said the prayer, and baptized him. He came up gasping for air. He said, "Elder Rasmussen, why did you hold me under so long?" I explained that he had not been under water more than three or four seconds. He said he saw his whole life flash before his eyes.

After the services we had a long, quiet ride back to Aabenraa. On subsequent visits to Brother Ravn, I learned that because of a heart condition, he had only taken sponge baths for the past several years. His doctor had told him never to go into water, because his heart would stop.

I finally realized why it had been so difficult to get him to recommit himself to baptism. To Brother Ravn, his baptism was going to be the ultimate commitment.

"Are you
a Mormon?"
Henry L. Isaksen

*W*e must frankly admit that there were many reasons for our move from Utah to Massachusetts several years ago— and that Christ's instructions to his disciples to teach the gospel to every creature was not the major factor in our decision. However, our experiences as a family of Mormons living in a non-LDS community have been rich and rewarding and have convinced us that the joys of missionary service are great and that they are available to every member of the Church—not just to the full-time missionaries. Let us illustrate.

Even before the two golden questions were proposed for general use by members of the Church, numerous opportunities presented themselves to each of us to refer names of interested people to the missionaries. Our second daughter was only ten years of age when we arrived at our new home. During the first few weeks of school she became the best friend of another girl in her class who inquired about the Church when she learned that we were from Utah. She and her mother were both interested enough to welcome the missionaries.

One of our young sons, age seven at the time, became acquainted with a girl from a neighboring community whose aunt and uncle are members of the Church. A friendship developed that has lasted now for several years and has contributed substantially to this girl's decision to join the Church even against the desires of her parents, who have finally given their consent for her baptism.

Our oldest daughter has invited many of her classmates (and some of her teachers) to attend Church services, youth activities, and cottage meetings with her and has thereby opened the doors of a number of homes to the missionaries. Likewise, as a college professor working with graduate students from various parts of the country, it has been my privilege to answer questions raised by them about the

Church and to refer the missionaries to the homes of those who have a desire to learn more.

One such student came to see me about his doctorate program, for which I was his adviser. After completing our business, he requested permission to ask me a personal question, and he said, "Are you a Mormon?"

I answered that I was, and he replied, "Well, I thought so! And from what I have seen of you, I figure that the teachings of your church are very close to my own beliefs. When can you tell me something about them?" My answer was to the effect that there was no time like the present.

During the hour that followed he seemed to drink in the various principles of the gospel as if he had just been waiting to hear about them. Nor was his thirst satisfied at the end of the hour. He responded enthusiastically to my suggestion that the missionaries call on him at his home and continue teaching him about the gospel. Several weeks later he came to me again after class and said, "The elders have been calling on us regularly every week, and I appreciate very much what they're doing to help us learn the gospel. But I'm impatient and have many unanswered questions that I'd like you to answer. When can you spend a couple of hours with me?" Needless to say, I found time very soon. He and his family have continued their investigation of the gospel and have expressed their intentions of joining the Church.

The importance of setting a good example, even when we are not aware that anyone is watching, has been brought home to us many times. Our oldest son, Hank, entered high school when we arrived, and he was soon recognized as someone who was different. At first there was a good deal of teasing about being such a good boy, and frequent attempts were made to get him to smoke a cigarette or take a drink. One boy even wagered that before the school year was over he could get Hank to break down and join them in their smoking and drinking.

Of course we were sure he would not, and the fact that he didn't was noticed not only by the boys but by their parents as well. This was borne out to me when I boarded a plane and found that I was sitting next to the father of one of my son's friends. He expressed his delight over their son's association with Hank and the fine example he was setting for all the boys in the neighborhood. A good gospel conversation ensued, which fortunately was prolonged for more than an hour beyond our scheduled landing time because of bad weather.

Yes, our son dated nonmember girls, and he attended social events sponsored by other religious groups. But we never doubted that he would remain true to the faith. Our confidence in him has been rewarded by his completion of a year at BYU and his acceptance of a mission call.

In addition to these informal missionary activities, Sister Isaksen had the opportunity to devote three evenings per week for a time (with the cooperation of the rest of the family) as a district missionary. Her companion was a recent convert—also the mother of a large family. Their efforts were rewarded in many ways, such as the baptism of an entire family: father, mother, and eight sons. How great will be their joy in the kingdom of God.

More recently the older children have been involved in the missionary program as members of a youth missionary committee. Their close association with the fine young men and women who are serving full-time missions in our area, as well as the missionary work itself, has been most rewarding. Each has had some interesting experiences with the two golden questions: What do you know about the Mormon Church? Would you like to know more?

Perhaps the most interesting experience, though, was one I had. The mother of a nonmember friend passed away, and I was asked to conduct the funeral services. By request, the services were brief, and I was the only speaker. The few words I spoke were based on the LDS concept of eternal life. As the minister, I was to ride from the chapel to the cemetery in the lead car with the funeral director. On the way he commented on the service and the wonderful philosophy upon which my remarks were based.

"Then it must be the first LDS service you've had in your establishment," I said.

He affirmed that it was. This seemed like an excellent opportunity to ask the golden questions.

"How much do you know about the Mormon Church?" I asked, ready to ask the second question regardless of his answer.

But it wasn't needed. His answer: "Not as much as I'd like to."

Yes, the joys of missionary service here in our non-LDS community are numerous for each member of the family. Needless to say, we miss the intimate contact with great numbers of fellow members and the opportunity to attend general conferences and temple sessions. But these and other experiences, too numerous to mention, more than compensate for the disadvantages of being away from the center of the Church. We have concluded that it does not matter, really, where we live. The important thing is to live close to the Lord and his church, and that can be done anywhere.

Instructor, October 1962, p. 359. Used by permission of the author.

The men
were masked

John Alexander

On the morning of the first of June, I left Brother Reed's about three miles from Adairsville, Georgia. . . . I told him I would go to Adairsville and see if I could make an appointment to preach, as we had never held any meetings in that neighborhood. I talked to a few farmers along the road, but the results were not satisfactory, and when about a mile from Adairsville I started to return to Brother Reed's.

About halfway between the two places, as I was singing aloud one of our hymns, I was startled by a noise and saw three masked men step out of a thicket and face me (the road here passed through a forest). This was about eleven o'clock in the morning. The men were masked by having what appeared to be some unbleached calico tied around their faces, under their eyes, and which hung down to their breasts. Their hats were pulled down over their foreheads to conceal the upper portions of their faces. One of the men was a slim man, over six feet high, I believe, who seemed the leader; the other two men were men of about five feet nine or ten inches.

When about ten feet from me, the tallest man said, "Are you one of those Mormon elders from Utah?" I told him I was. He replied, "You go up there in the brush."

I answered, "I don't feel like going up. What do you want me to go for?"

At this he blurted out, "You go. I won't tell you again."

He then drew his pistol and covered me. The other two followed his example. I walked into the brush fifty yards the way they pointed. Then I stopped and turned around. The leader told me to go on. I told him I had gone as far as I was going. At this they drew their pistols and presented them at my face, about four feet off. I then turned to start up the hill again, when the leader gave me the first kick that threw me on my hands and knees. I raised myself and struck at him, but he was downhill, and I missed him and struck a small tree, fell flat on the ground, and rolled onto my side. Just as I fell, one of the others, who was above me on the hill, ran three or four steps toward me and jumped on my stomach. Just as I was getting up, the third one kicked me in the left side. I then started up the hill, very slowly, because of my great pain. When I had again gone about one hundred and fifty yards I made the last stop; I turned around and said, "For God's sake, men, you don't mean to kill a young, innocent man. What have I done?"

The leader answered, "Well, you, you came out here preaching false doctrine, and you know it's false, and say that it is."

I replied, "No, sir, I don't think it's false; I know it is not false, and I can't say that it is."

He said, "Well, you're going to die right here; have you anything to say?" I told him if they meant to kill me, I had something to say. He continued, "Well, what is it?"

I asked him, "Will you allow me to offer up a few words of prayer?"

"Yes," he said, "if you'll be quick about it."

I . . . said, "Oh, my God, if it is thy will that these men should take my life, I am willing to die," and a few more words that I do not recollect. I then . . . looked them straight in the face.

As they lowered their pistols, one pointing to my face, another lower, I closed my eyes. The moment my eyes closed, three shots were fired. I recollect hearing the reports, but nothing after. My senses seemed taken away. I felt myself falling but do not recollect striking the ground.

When I came to, the first thing I remember was that I was on my hands and knees looking around. I arose to my feet. I ran, or rather staggered or stumbled, down to the road. I did not know which way I was going or where I was going, but I kept on until I found myself at Brother Reed's fence; that was the first time I realized where I was. I there fell exhausted, and Brother Reed came, picked me up, and carried me into the house. In about half an hour, I think, I came around so that I could talk to him. I believe it was about noon when I reached Brother Reed's. Brother Reed and his family took the greatest care of me.

My traveling companion, Brother Orson M. Wilson, of Hyrum, Cache County, came to me the next evening. On Sunday, Brothers Barber and Parrish came with a buggy, and about two o'clock (they having held a meeting at Brother Reed's in the morning) we started for Brother Barber's home at Heywood, about sixteen miles distant. They left me at Brother Smith's in Heywood until Wednesday, when Brother Barber took me to Rome, about fifteen miles away, and on the evening train Brother Parrish started for Chattanooga with me.

Of the three shots, one went through the front of my hat (a low-crowned, black and white straw). As I was a little up the hill and the hat was slightly tilted back, the ball went in at the front and almost immediately came out of the crown, giving the appearance of glancing upwards. This was the shot fired by the leader, who I noticed had his pistol pointed at my head. My coat was rather open, and the second bullet passed through it on the left side, just grazing the slide of my watch chain. The third ball did not touch me.

When the three men shot, they were standing in a row about twelve steps from me.

Juvenile Instructor, vol. 18 (1883), p. 207

"I have a great gift to give you"

Alice Colton Smith

*I*n a beautiful European city, a young and earnest branch president told the Saints that President David O. McKay had asked each member to be a missionary and to bring one convert into the Church each year. After the service, a blind sister came forward tearfully and asked, "How can I do this? I am old and cannot see. I have been in the Church many years. I have no friends who are not members. How can I bring anyone into the Church?"

The branch president said, "Sister, if you have faith and a desire to do his will, God will show you the way."

Some weeks later, this sister was traveling on a train. During the journey, the passengers who sat opposite her helped with her luggage and cared for her needs with special compassion for her affliction. The sister thought, "What can I do to repay them?" In a few moments she leaned across and said, "I want to give you something for your kindness. I have a great gift to give you, if you will accept it."

The new friends smiled. How could this woman, obviously not well-off, give them a great gift? Politely, they thanked her and said it wasn't necessary. She gently persisted. One of the women finally said, "I will be glad to accept it."

The member sister replied, "This gift is not of money or jewelry; it is a gift of the Holy Spirit. I know that God lives. I know that Jesus is the Christ. I know that living on the earth today is one of God's prophets who reveals to us the word of God. This great gift of knowledge I can give to you."

The woman, interested in spite of the odd situation, asked, "How?"

"Give me your address and I will send to you two young men who will explain." This was done.

Three years later the elderly blind woman made her way down the church aisle to ask the mission president, "President, how many people have I helped to bring into the Church by now?"

Tears streamed down her face as he answered, "Your faith has helped in bringing eight souls into the Church—the woman you met and seven of her friends and relatives."

True conversion requires us to repent of our lack of faith, to be humble, to share the gospel with others, and to try to do the will of our Father in heaven all of our days.

Illogical deduction

Karl G. Maeser belonged to a high rank and caste that Mormonism is seldom able to reach, even under ideal circumstances. In this case it was accomplished under almost impossible conditions. At the age of eleven, he was blind for eight months. At twenty-one he taught high school. When he married the daughter of the director of the Budich Institute in Dresden June 11, 1854, it was considered a union of the two most prominent families in town. At age twenty-six he became the assistant director of the Budich Institute. He found himself at the top of the social scale and caught up with materialistic philosophy that was becoming so popular among scholars of the day.

It was in 1854 that Dr. Maeser came across a tract written by an anti-Mormon writer. "His illogical deductions aroused my curiosity," the German scholar later related. In another publication he read that the Mormons had a mission headquarters in Copenhagen and the mission president's name was given. The German educator had an agent trace the address of the mission president and wrote to him requesting more information. The Scandinavian Mission president, John Van Cott, wrote back saying that neither he nor his secretary knew a word of German and suggesting that Maeser write to the Swiss Mission in Geneva, where Daniel Tyler was the mission president. When Dr. Maeser did this, he was again disappointed. One of the elders advised President Tyler not to answer the letter, "because the Germans are probably trying to discover the activities the Mormons are carrying on in their country." President Tyler returned the letter unanswered. Dr. Maeser was so offended and angered that he sent another letter to President Van Cott in Denmark, who this time found someone who could read German and then wrote to President Tyler in Switzerland urging him to correspond with the German. After several letters were exchanged, Dr. Maeser requested that an elder be sent to him.

On Friday, September 28, 1854, a British missionary, William Budge, arrived in Dresden. He did not know a word of German and was allowed into the country only as an English instructor. As a precautionary measure, he had sent Maeser half a zigzag-cut card, so that he could match it up with the other half when the two met—a safeguard against meeting the wrong person.

Foreign missionaries were outlawed in Saxony at this time, and the atmosphere was very tense with political unrest. Dr. Maeser did not know a word of English. The two communicated by opening up both an English and a German Bible, and Elder Budge would point out the scriptures he wanted Maeser to read. Dr. Maeser later related, "Although we could not understand each other, my family and I were most impressed with his personality and sincerity."

William Budge learned German exceedingly fast. On October 11, when the European Mission president, Franklin D. Richards, and William Kimball, son of Heber C. Kimball, arrived, Elder Budge was able to act as interpreter. At midnight, two miles out of Dresden in the Elbe River, the first Mormon baptisms in the kingdom of Saxony were performed by Elder Richards. Dr. Maeser later related that when he came out of the water, "I lifted both hands to the heavens and said, 'Father, if you approve of what I have done, give me a sign, and whatsoever thou requirest of me I will do, even the giving of my life.' " The group separated to go back to Dresden, so as not to arouse suspicion. President Richards and Karl Maeser were walking together conversing, with Elder Budge acting as interpreter. Then, according to Dr. Maeser's own account, "I found myself answering the questions in German that President Richards had asked in English without Brother Budge's interpretation, and President Richards could understand me without an interpreter also." Karl G. Maeser believed he had received his sign, because in succeeding days they again needed someone to translate. A week later the families of Dr. Maeser and two men who had joined the Church with him were baptized, bringing the number of converts at this time to nine.

———————————

Gilbert Scharffs, *Mormonism in Germany* (Deseret Book Co., 1970), p. 16.

*V*aea Aiatia from Solosolo, Upolu, Western Samoa, was baptized July 24, 1970. He was the only member of The Church of Jesus Christ of Latter-day Saints in his village. He attended meetings in Eva, Upolu, which was about four miles from his village. Because of transportation problems, he usually had to walk the distance. Each time we went to his home, we received a warm greeting and a spiritual feeling. We had hoped that, through Vaea, we could baptize the whole family.

Vaea's mother, Sa'a Tupau Aiatia, and her family asked us to bless her. She had been blind since 1964. Various medicines had been tried with no success. We fasted for two days and entered their home on Thursday. We were greeted by two chiefs and four other members of the family, all of whom were non-Mormons except Vaea. We talked for three hours about the gospel and the Prophet Joseph Smith. We explained the purpose for our visit, and they replied, to our astonishment, that they realized the reason and they too had been fasting for two days. I felt so proud to know that these people realized that we held the priesthood of God. We knelt around Sa'a as she sat cross-legged on the floor. Elder Hathaway anointed her and I sealed the anointing and gave her a blessing. I blessed her that she would receive physical sight and also spiritual sight. I felt a warm spirit, and when we arose, there were tear-filled eyes, and many thank-you's were exchanged.

We returned often to check on Sa'a, but no physical sight came. One day as we visited the family, she asked us to give her the lessons. For the second discussion we used the Bible and Book of Mormon to explain the relationship of Lehi and the two books of scripture. We made Sa'a put her hands on each book, and as we talked we touched her hands. We used rocks, wire, paper, and whatever was available to help illustrate the message. As we referred to one object or the other, Sa'a would move her hands over the objects, recalling the story and asking questions. She radiated a warm, burning witness, and we could feel that she was receiving the message. As we continued with other lessons, her family was persecuted more and more by villagers, but Vaea and Sa'a kept their special spirits burning.

Elder Hathaway was transferred and Elder Byron Chappell became my new companion. Four miles is a long way in Samoa, where the terrain is rough and few buses pass on Sunday. How could we ever get Sa'a those four miles to church? Through prayer and fasting it was finally decided that the zone leader would pick up Vaea and Sa'a on Sunday. She was very impressed with the service and wanted baptism. We worked with her a couple more weeks and let her attend church in Eva. She was so excited the day we set her baptism for September 18, 1970.

I was transferred the day before her baptism. I felt very let down, but Sa'a assured me that the baptism would take place, and we bid farewell. Elder Chappell told me that the services were very spiritual, and at the end Sa'a stood up with tears in her eyes and gave thanks to God and bore her testimony.

I left the mission field shortly after that. Elder Chappell worked with the family for several months, and he said that the rest of the family was beginning to receive the discussions. About a year after that, I received word that one of the chiefs who was present at Sa'a's blessing had joined the Church along with his wife and children.

I have yet to meet another person with such a radiating spirit as that blind Samoan lady, Sa'a Tupau Aiatia.

"My day was filled with sunshine"
Grace Montgomery

*O*ne sunny day in October 1964, I was caring for a lady seventy-two years of age. She was a nice person, but she had upset me, and I was quite agitated.

Then the doorbell rang. A young man was there, and he told me that he was an elder from The Church of Jesus Christ of Latter-day Saints. He asked if he could call again and talk with me. I agreed, and gave him my name and address.

After he left, my day was filled with sunshine, and I couldn't get him out of my mind. I felt something wonderful taking place inside me, and everything went smoothly the rest of the day.

The young man called back, bringing with him another elder. They invited me to church, and there I found what I had been looking for. I had attended many churches, but I couldn't seem to get anything out of any of them. I knew that the LDS Church was right for me, and I decided I wanted to be baptized as soon as possible.

Since I met the missionaries, God has shown me the light and brought me out of the darkness. They are very special to me. Without their help and teaching, I would probably have drifted along and never known the true gospel of Jesus Christ. I wouldn't give up what I received through those two young men for all the world. I will always thank my Heavenly Father for sending them to me. Now that I have been baptized, I have something to hold on to, something to live for. My eyes are open to the true gospel.

One ward discovers
missionary work

Lindsay R. Curtis

Paula and Glenda had somehow figured out a way to be on the picnic bus carrying servicemen from Hill Air Force Base. But they were not going just for the picnic—not Paula and Glenda. They had accepted their bishop's challenge and were well on their way to the promise he had given them at the same time.

In their interview with their bishop of the student ward in Ogden, Utah, they were challenged to fast, praying that the Lord make known the individuals they were to bring into the Church. They were promised that if they would place themselves in tune with the Spirit, the Lord would indeed point his finger in the direction they were to go.

To Paula and Glenda, the answer to their prayers was clear; those whom they should seek to influence were the young servicemen at Hill Air Force Base. As they searched for a way to meet them, the picnic came along, and so did Paula and Glenda. By the end of the picnic, Paula and Glenda had arranged for several of the young men on the bus to meet with the missionaries.

This was to be the beginning of a seemingly never-ending chain of conversions as many young men from the base came into the Church that summer.

"Now think carefully," the bishop said. "Are you certain there are no nonmembers among all of your friends?"

"Well, yes; there is one," Lynne hesitated. "But I don't think he would ever become a member of our church."

"You fast and pray about it," the bishop challenged. "If the Spirit moves you, bring him to the fireside next Sunday."

Bill showed up with Lynne the following Sunday, and after a very spiritual discussion, a ward member approached him: "Bill, have you ever really had the opportunity to hear the story of the Mormons?"

"I've heard a little about them," Bill answered.

"How would you like to spend the most interesting

evening you've ever had and hear the most exciting story you've ever heard?" asked one of the members. Bill not only listened to this exciting story but joined the Church as well. He recently returned from a very successful mission.

Jan was teaching school while attending the student ward. "Bishop," she said, "I want to do missionary work too, but I have no contacts outside of my students."

"The challenge and the promise apply to everyone," the bishop replied. "The president of the Church has given everyone the charge to be a missionary. Give the Lord the opportunity to bless you, and see if he won't point his finger to that one with whom you should share the message."

The challenge came within a few days in the form of one of her students who needed counsel. Jan's counseling was subsequently extended to the girl's mother and resulted in the mother and her two daughters joining the Church.

"I took the challenge, bishop, and I know who the person is. But now what do I say to him?" asked Bert.

"You might ask the Lord to tell you what to say. And you can always ask if he has heard the real story of the Mormons. You know, many people have lived among us for years and have never really heard our story. And yet our message is the most exciting news on earth—that the Lord has spoken again!"

But Bert's contact turned him down. Completely disheartened, he returned to the bishop, his confidence badly shaken.

"Tell me one thing," the bishop asked, "did you really love that person, or was he just a statistic? It's impossible to carry the message of the restored gospel successfully unless your heart is filled with love. Go back and fast and pray until you feel completely in tune with the Spirit and until your heart is filled with love for that person. Then approach him again."

This time the young man accepted the invitation to meet with the missionaries. Not only was he baptized into the Church, but his wife also became active in the Church again, and their two children will now be reared in a gospel home.

Mike, a young returned missionary, had had few baptisms in Norway, but he was now in charge of the gymnasium at Hill Air Force Base, and the bishop felt impressed that Mike might have a special mission in the ward. After fasting and praying, Mike received the same feeling. Each week he brought one or two young men he had met at the gymnasium to ward activities or to sacrament meeting. They were quickly fellowshipped into the ward, and many met with the missionaries. A continuing stream of conversions has followed.

After Mike left the service to attend Utah State University, he met Monte, a graduate student who had never been approached by anyone from the Church during all his years at the university. He was almost waiting for an invitation to hear about the Church. He was baptized a month after he met Mike. As far as finding "golden contacts" was concerned, Mike's mission had just begun.

Jerry had also met Mike at the gymnasium. Along with a buddy, George, he came to a ward activity and, at his baptism, lamented that he had spent eight full months in the service before he heard of the gospel. "Why couldn't I have heard about it sooner?" he asked.

Jerry went to Vietnam, and during his tour of duty he was inexplicably transferred for one month to Korea. While he was gone, his section of the barracks was blown up; he would have been killed had he still been in Vietnam. Discharged early because of his father's death, Jerry was called by his home branch to serve a mission to the Philippines. He has since returned, baptized his mother, and is now serving as branch president in Statesville, North Carolina.

Meanwhile, George was also baptized and later married in the temple.

The ward averaged about a baptism a week, with the new converts constantly infusing their newfound faith and zeal into the other members of the ward. This same priceless spirituality is found wherever people actively share the gospel.

Several things are necessary, however, to make such a program successful. First of all, there must be capable, dedicated, spiritual missionaries. Our ward was blessed with them.

Second, a bishop has the privilege of issuing both a challenge to share the gospel and the promise that the Lord will answer prayers and direct missionaries to those who will hear. Every time a bishop interviews a ward member for an award, for an advancement, for a position, for a temple recommend, or for tithing settlement, the privilege is always there—to end that interview on a high spiritual note with a challenge and a promise.

Lastly, the members must make the challenge a matter of fasting and prayer. In tune with the Spirit of the Lord, they can be prompted where to look, what to say. And if they truly love their fellowmen, it will show in their countenance, and those approached will recognize this and respond.

Here's the challenge: Have you ever really heard the story of the Mormons? If you would like to spend the greatest evening of your life, I have two friends who would love to tell it to you.

The Lord himself makes the promise: "And now, if your joy will be great with one soul that you have brought unto me into the kingdom of my Father, how great will be your joy if you should bring many souls unto me!" (D&C 18:16.)

Ensign, March 1975, p. 21. Used by permission of the author.

You can afford
to be patient

Benjamin E. Rich

*T*hat Elder Rich did not court debate, and did not believe in tearing down the religious faiths of others, is seen in a bit of advice given his elders while presiding over the Southern States Mission:

"Do not be anxious to engage in the work of tearing down other churches, but devote yourselves to explaining the gospel in plainness and simplicity. Point to the beauties of the principles and the perfection of the organization. When you have done this, under the influence of the Holy Spirit, the honest in heart will see before them a vision of such a heavenly temple that they will admit in their hearts it is a better house than the one in which they now dwell, and then mankind will be more willing to come unto that building and take up their abode. . . . You can afford to be patient because you are the followers of a Master who was the very embodiment of patience, and you can afford to be brave because you are clothed with the power of God and his holy priesthood."

Thomas C. Romney, *The Gospel in Action* (Salt Lake City: Deseret Sunday School Union Board, 1949), p. 183.

"I know the Mormon Church is true"

Robert Carpenter

Early in December 1974, Elder Brad Smith and I decided to call some people we hadn't contacted for some time. As usual, most of them weren't very enthusiastic about making an appointment with us. However, one man named Rick Bowne said, "Come on over. I'd like to talk to you." We went to his home that very afternoon.

As we drove up to a huge home with a lake in back, I thought to myself, "These people are probably more interested in money than anything else."

They invited us in and were very friendly. Rick is a geologist and his wife, Laura, is a chemist. We showed them the filmstrip *Ancient America Speaks,* which really interested them. Then we presented the first discussion. They were fairly receptive, and we were able to make a return appointment. However, Laura told us she was active in the Methodist Church and had no intention of changing.

The following Wednesday we taught them the second discussion, which concerns the plan of salvation. It went pretty well because they had both been reading and praying.

When we returned the next week, they told us they believed in evolution, and if we didn't believe in it, we might as well leave. We told them we would talk about that subject later, and we presented the next discussion. Before we left we had a return appointment and a commitment that they would come to church.

The Bownes were unable to keep either commitment because Laura's younger sister died unexpectedly, and they had to go to Ohio for the funeral. I called them when they returned, and they asked us to come right over. When we got there, they were pretty tired from their long trip. We could tell that they were upset about the death. They asked us many questions about life after death and listened intently to every word we said.

After answering their questions, we started teaching them the sixth discussion, which concerns our relationship to

Christ. About halfway through the lesson Laura stopped us and said, "I don't know if this sounds unusual or not, and I don't mean to interrupt, but I know the Mormon Church is true."

She went on to explain that while we were talking about Christ's visit to America, a sweet, peaceful feeling came over her, a kind of burning in her heart that she didn't know how to describe.

We explained that it was the Holy Ghost witnessing to her the truthfulness of the gospel. Then we asked Rick how he felt. He said that he felt good about the gospel and hoped it was true, but he wanted to be sure.

We had prayer and challenged them to be baptized the next Saturday, two days later. Laura said, "I know I'm ready. I hope Rick will be also."

The zone leaders came over to the Bownes' home the next evening to interview them, and the baptism was set for 7:30 Saturday evening.

At 7:35 that Saturday one of the elders and I were pacing the floor, hoping Rick hadn't backed out. Finally, at 7:40 they arrived. They had had trouble finding the chapel.

We had called some of the ward members, so there was a large group present for the baptism. The members warmly welcomed the Bownes. The baptismal service was beautiful and the spirit was strong.

For a while Rick still had some doubts, but he also had a great deal of faith. Today, after being members for five months, both Rick and Laura have strong testimonies and hold positions of responsibility in the ward.

"He took me
for a cotton picker"

John Brown

I set out alone on Sunday the 27th, crossed the Tennessee River on a bridge at Florence, passed through Tuscumbia, and stopped at the gate of Mr. Hyde, who kept a stand on the road two miles from the latter place. I hailed, and Mr. Hyde, who was at supper, came out. I told him I was traveling, without purse or scrip, for the purpose of preaching the gospel, and I would be thankful if he could keep me overnight and give me something to eat.

My appearance and address rather puzzled him. I appeared to be a lad about seventeen and rather poorly clad. He took me for a cotton picker trying to pass as a preacher to save expenses. It was the season of the year when the poorer class of Tennessee, who farmed on a small scale, went to the more southern districts to pick cotton. He finally replied that he would rather hear me inquiring for employment. I asked him if they did not believe in preaching and worshiping God in that country. He replied, "Oh! yes," and with a smile between insignificance and surprise, he told me I could stay but he would call on me to preach. I replied, "I will, most cheerfully, if you will gather a congregation." He said there were some strangers stopping with him and they and his family would make a congregation.

The contract being made, he opened the gate and invited me into the yard and to a seat on a chair under a shade tree in front of the house, where he and his friends had been enjoying themselves.

He went into the house chuckling and snickering at the anticipated sport of hearing a stripling of a cotton picker preach. He related the whole to his friends and family, who joined in with anticipation of great sport. It was now dark and I was invited in to supper. I ate very heartily of sweet potatoes, sliced pie, etc., after which, all preliminaries being arranged, Mr. Hyde assembled his congregation, which consisted of his family, four or five horse drivers, and a Mr. Steel, who kept a tavern fifteen miles down the road south.

183

A lighted candle and family Bible were placed upon the table. I was then called upon to fill my part of the contract. I took my seat by the table, picked up the Bible, and opened it. I looked around upon the congregation, all of whom had cast their eyes downward, not daring to look at each other for fear of not being able to keep from laughing. My appearance (as a cotton picker) and my singular introduction (as a preacher) was as much as they could endure and observe good behavior. I sang a hymn without any assistance, although solicited, after which I kneeled down to pray. No one else moved from his seat. After prayer I arose and looked over the congregation but could not catch an eye. I commenced speaking upon the first principles of the gospel, and the Lord gave me his Spirit in a powerful manner. In less than five minutes all eyes were upon me, and the congregation was as motionless as statues of marble. But for the sound of my voice, the dropping of a pin could be heard in any part of the room for three-quarters of an hour.

After my remarks, I dismissed the meeting in regular order. But before I was seated or any person had time to move, Mr. Hyde told me not to leave in the morning without breakfast, and Mr. Steel very politely invited me to take dinner with him the next day.

They knew nothing of the Mormon elders; consequently it was all new to them. I was very reserved till after meeting, calculating to make their surprise as great as possible. Next day, August 28, I called on Mr. Steel, who received me with smiles of friendship. He had gone home by stage in the night. He gave me all the particulars of the anticipated fun with the supposed "cotton picker" the evening before. He said, "You came off with flying colors." I took dinner with him and then pursued my journey, walking thirty-two miles that day.

John Z. Brown, *Autobiography of Pioneer John Brown* (Salt Lake City: Stevens & Wallis, Inc., 1941), p. 42.

"I have seven more sons"

Castle H. Murphy

*E*lder Kirkham lost his life on east Maui as the car in which he was riding left the winding road and plunged into the gulch below. We were all heavyhearted, realizing what this would mean to the family of this fine missionary. We learned later that when the body was being lowered over the ship's side at San Francisco, the father stood waiting to receive it to his home state for interment. A gentleman who had heard of the sad passing stepped up to him and asked, "How can you believe in a God who would permit such a thing to happen to your son while he was actually and busily engaged in preaching the gospel at such great sacrifice to all concerned?"

The father, though heartbroken, replied, "Well, sir, my heart is heavy, and I don't know how his mother will stand it, but I have seven more sons, and I would be happy if each one of them could end his life as did this fine boy—in the service of the Master."

"Greater love hath no man than this, that he lay down his life for his friends."

Castle H. Murphy, *Castle of Zion—Hawaii* (Deseret Book Co., 1963), p. 23.

The beginnings
in Thailand
Craig G. Christensen

On November 2, 1966, Elder Gordon B. Hinckley of the Council of the Twelve and a small group of Latter-day Saints from the Bangkok Branch assembled in Bangkok's Lumpini Park for the dedication of Thailand for the preaching of the gospel. Subsequently, there followed a more than two-year struggle through the seemingly endless channels of Asian bureaucracy before the Church was incorporated in Thailand November 1, 1967.

Upon receiving approval from the First Presidency, and under the direction of President Keith B. Garner of the Southern Far East Mission, a vanguard of six elders arrived in Bangkok on February 2, 1968. A home to serve as their living quarters was secured in the Bangkaoi section on Sukumvit Road.

On Monday, February 5, President Garner returned to the mission headquarters in Hong Kong. His instructions to the missionaries were short and explicit: learn the Thai language and arrange to have the six missionary discussions translated.

At the date of their arrival, there was no Church literature in the Thai language; not even the name of the Church had been translated. The elders relied on fasting and prayer for guidance. Within one week a translator for the six discussions had been employed, and a language school with Thai instructors had been located. Then began three weeks of intensive instruction in the Thai language. In the evenings, time was utilized by tracting in the *farang* (foreign) areas of Bangkok. The reactions of most Occidentals to the undertaking ranged from scorn to pity. "Your failure is assured," the elders were told. "The Thais have a religion that is perfectly suited to them. Don't try to change a contented people with your western religion."

The thrust of these opinions was amplified when it was learned that the first Protestant missionaries in Thailand had labored thirty-seven years before baptizing their first

186

convert. Only in recent years had the entire Bible been available in a Thai translation, and it had many flaws. According to estimates, 97 percent of Thailand is Buddhist, with the remaining portion divided among the Islam, Catholic, Protestant, and Hindu faiths.

The first crucial weeks were accompanied with a special blessing: a young Thai man, Anan Eldredge, who had been adopted by an American Latter-day Saint family living in Thailand and had been subsequently baptized, was sent to live with the elders to help them learn the language. With his help, they were able to conduct the first Latter-day Saint services entirely in the Thai language in a mere five weeks after their arrival in Thailand. Six Thai investigators were present. (At this writing, Brother Anan, now an elder, is serving as the first full-time native missionary in Thailand.)

The pressures and frustrations of the initial weeks were made more endurable through the meeting of a very special individual. Dr. Gordon Flammer of the Bangkok Branch introduced the elders to an intelligent Thai gentleman and his wife, Boonepluke and Rabiab Klaophin. Mr. Boonepluke (Thais use the first name almost exclusively) was employed at the school where Dr. Flammer taught and had expressed interest in the Church because of his observation of the habits and characteristics of its members.

Mr. Boonepluke had taught himself enough English to communicate on a fairly technical level, so the missionaries began to teach him the six discussions in English, and he in turn would translate for his wife. These meetings were very spiritual experiences. His desire to learn the gospel was intense. He literally memorized each point in the discussions and made certain he had thoroughly digested the material in each lesson before proceeding to the next. He understood the significance of prayer and made certain that his family had daily prayers. He became a regular attendee at the weekly meetings held in the elders' home. Attendance meant a one-hour motorcycle ride with his wife and two children through the crowded streets of Bangkok. His punctuality in a land where time is considered only in terms of early and late was truly commendable. At length, Brother Boonepluke and his wife were challenged to be baptized.

Space does not allow a discussion of the ramifications of the Thai social structure. Suffice it to say that a Thai man who rejects Buddhism is looked upon as somewhat of a traitor, because Buddhism and the Thai government are inextricably related historically, ceremonially, and philosophically. Such a person becomes a social outcast in many circles and is almost certain to bring disgrace upon his family. Nevertheless, after much personal prayer and counsel from the missionaries, Brother Boonepluke and his wife were baptized and confirmed members of the Church on May 15, 1968. It was the first baptismal service held by the missionaries in Thailand. (When I left Thailand nine months later, he was serving as a counselor in the Bangkok Thai Branch.)

It is obviously impossible to give a detailed account of the conversion of each member, but there are two others whose roles in the establishment of the Church in Thailand should be noted. Brother Prasong Sriveses, who was employed by the Thailand District president, Eugene P. Till, listened to the six discussions in "pidgin" Thai (as then spoken by the elders) with a degree of comprehension that can only be explained as a gift of the Holy Ghost. Brother Prasong was baptized on June 12, 1968, and the following week he was ordained a priest and set apart as an assistant in the Sunday School superintendency.

A few weeks after arriving in Bangkok, two of the elders met an extraordinary lady, Mrs. Srilaksanaa. Of noble ancestry, she was well-educated and had traveled extensively. She consented to listen to the discussions, and through prayer and study of the Book of Mormon, she gained a fervent testimony; she and her two daughters were baptized July 4, 1968. Since that time, her eloquence and strong testimony have been invaluable in the conversion of other Thai people. She has served the Church as a teacher of an investigators class and has assisted in translation work.

In June 1968 President Garner was in Bangkok in conjunction with a district conference and was inspired to send two elders to the city of Nakorn Rajasima, better known as Korat, to begin missionary work. They arrived on June 21, and the following week regular Sunday meetings were started. Brother Anan Eldredge and his family were then living in Korat, and he was again invaluable in starting the work there. Korat, the third largest city in Thailand, has a population of about 75,000. From the beginning, there was a special spirit there, and the hand of the Lord was evident countless times in the locating and conversion of those souls whom he had prepared to receive the gospel. Within a short time the Korat group had about thirty regular attendees, and baptismal services were held monthly. The converts were from all walks of life: students, military men, common laborers, and two former Protestant ministers. The circumstances of their conversions were almost without exception dramatic and miraculous. In a few months it was necessary to find a larger meeting place.

The elders have found it to be a choice experience to work among the Thais. Their warmth and sincerity are unmatched anywhere. They are quick to make friends and are generally humble and content with their lives. They are quick to smile and slow to anger. One who is acquainted with the Polynesian temperament would not find it difficult to understand the Thais. However, the Thais are tolerant of religions to an unnerving degree; thus attempts to teach any one set of beliefs are very often unfruitful. This particular difficulty will likely be unsettling to missionaries in Thailand for years to come.

In July 1968 President Garner was released, and W. Brent Hardy was set apart as the new mission president. Under his direction, the elders then laboring in Bangkok were assigned to revise and correct the then existing translations of the six missionary lessons. This proved to be a ponderous task, for the native Thai translators who had been hired were faced with two major problems: (1) they were not familiar with the Church terminology and doctrine, and (2) the Thai language makes no provision for Christian concepts. For example, *Savior* must be translated as "the Holy One who helps." To date, no suitable equivalent for the word *priesthood* has been discovered or coined. Thus, after only eight months in Thailand, the Church was established in two cities, the six missionary discussions had been suitably translated, and a good translation of "Joseph Smith's Testimony" was ready for publication.

In December 1968, Elder Ezra Taft Benson of the Council of the Twelve visited Bangkok to attend a quarterly district conference. During his visit, he was granted an audience with the king of Thailand, and he presented him with a copy of the Book of Mormon and a Thai language copy of "Joseph Smith's Testimony."

During that same district conference, President Hardy instructed two pairs of missonary companions to travel throughout northern Thailand, in order to determine which cities might be suitable for missionary work. In the northern provinces of Thailand dwell several hill tribes whose culture, language, and traditions differ markedly from the Thais who inhabit the lowlands. The elders had heard of a tape recording that described some of these traditions. The following is taken from the journal of one of the missionaries, Elder Alan H. Hess:

"After a while we decided to go in search of the people who sold the Karen hill tribe music tapes. All seemed to go without a hitch. The post office gave us the address of the post office box number we had received. When we got to the place, we found it to be the Baptist Mission. They have done extensive work among the hill tribes. They were quite curious as to why we wanted the tape, but they sold it to us anyway. Later we went into a tape recording shop and played it. The narrator told how the Karens have a legend about a golden book which was given to their forefathers. They say that they lost this 'Book of Life' through negligence. They also say that some white men will bring it to them again. Here is the narration as taken from the tape: 'The story of the Golden Book of Life has a large place in the traditions of the Karens. After Creation, God sojourned with man for a while, then returned to heaven to the company of his youngest son, a white man. Upon arriving in heaven, God gave the white man three books of life, one each for his children on earth. The books were delivered, and the white brother took his leave to the west, promising to pay a return visit someday. However, the Karen Indians soon lost their golden book through negligence and began wandering the pathway of animistic fears. With fervent expectation and hope, the Karen looks for the coming of his white brothers with the Golden Book of Life.' This longing helped open the way for early Christian missionaries. It is little wonder that the Bible has become the touchstone of the Karen Church and its faith."

The following is a translation of a chant that has been handed down through the centuries among these hill tribes:

"The old men tell us, 'Children remember this:
Remember that the white foreigner will return the Golden Book.
When that happens, take the book, and take care of it.
If you don't it'll be lost, and then there will be no hope at all.
We're old, it's too late for us, but you'll be there.
Watch the sea for the big ship.
Where the waves beat themselves white,
Watch for the white man's ship.
They'll have the golden book.
Take it.' "

Continuing the journal excerpts:

"Upon arrival in Chiang Mai we were speaking with some of the taxi drivers and one of them gave us the name of a Mr. Thompson, who was from the Karen tribe, but was taken when just a child and brought up by Baptist missionaries. He works in a local bank, and is active in the Baptist Church. The Lord was really with us in that almost as soon as we arrived back at the hotel, one of the workers there came to our door; and even before we asked, she said she knew where Mr. Thompson lived and offered to take us there. We went with this little lady on a bus and up a road on the other end of town that would have been almost impossible for us to find on our own. Mr. Thompson received us most kindly and, upon request, related the tribe legend to us a little bit differently than we had heard it before. He said there was a gold book and a silver book which had been lost. The Baptists had been teaching that one book was the Bible and one was the hymnbook. We told him about Joseph Smith, the gold plates, and the story of the Book of Mormon. He seemed impressed, but didn't really understand the import. But he did agree to pray about it. And we told him we would go to his bank the following day and take him a Book of Mormon."

As one who witnessed the opening pages of the history of the Church in Thailand, I believe that there is every reason to believe that the words of Elder Hinckley in his dedicatory prayer will be fulfilled, and tens of thousands of Thai people will one day become members of The Church of Jesus Christ of Latter-day Saints.

Improvement Era, March 1970, p. 32. Used by permission of the author.

"Tell him not to trouble"

Lorenzo Snow

*I*n the spring of 1840, Elder Snow was called on a mission to England. Before his departure he called on a number of the wives of the apostles laboring in England to gather what messages he should bear to their husbands. He found President Brigham Young's wife living in an unfinished log cabin with loose boards on the floor and no chinking between the logs, leaving the family exposed to wind and storm. She had just returned from a fruitless search for a milk cow that had strayed away the day before and on which the family depended for milk.

"On asking her what she wished me to say to her husband," recalls Lorenzo, "she replied, 'You see my situation, but tell him not to trouble or worry in the least about me—I wish him to remain in his field of labor until honorably released.' "

Then Elder Snow commented: "Her apparent poverty-stricken, destitute condition deeply stirred my sympathy. I had but little money—not sufficient to take me one-tenth the distance to my field of labor, with no prospects of obtaining the balance, and was then on the eve of starting. I drew from my pocket a portion of my small pittance and presented it to her, but she refused to accept it. While I strenuously insisted on her taking it, and partly accidentally, the money was dropped on the floor and rattled through the openings between the loose boards, which settled the dispute. Bidding her goodbye, I left her to pick it up at her leisure."

Eliza R. Snow, *Biography and Family Record of Lorenzo Snow* (Salt Lake City: Deseret News Company, 1884), p. 47.

The power
of example

Castle H. Murphy

Sister Murphy and I were invited to a dinner at the home of one of our friends. The contacts made there were very pleasant to us, and the evening moved on very agreeably until we were called to the dinner table. The table was beautiful, the food was delicious, and the group was jovial and happy. As the meal progressed, coffee was poured into the cups at each place without anyone asking if we cared to drink it. Both Verna and I proceeded to partake of the food without any comment as to the coffee, but those seated near us and the host urged us to taste the coffee. Still we did not partake. They became persistent, but finally desisted and brought us milk to drink. Without further comment as to coffee drinking, the guests left the table and retired to the living room for further conversation, which was all very pleasant.

When we retired, it did not occur to us that there was anything out of place or unusual at the party. However, the next morning at an early hour, our next-door neighbor who, with her fine husband (a nonmember), had been in attendance at the dinner the evening before, knocked on our door. We arose and admitted her. She began by saying that we would never know how important it was to her that we had not partaken of the offered coffee the previous night. She said that the dinner was really arranged on a wager that, if all others touched the coffee, we would, even though we had just returned from the mission field.

"My husband said that if you did drink the beverage, he would no longer have any interest in joining the Church. But now that he knows you resist such temptations, he will further continue his investigation of the gospel."

We were very happy about this.

Soon after this incident this good woman's husband applied for baptism and became a very useful church worker.

194

Few have done more in temple work and genealogical research.

Castle H. Murphy, *Castle of Zion—Hawaii* (Salt Lake City:Deseret Book Co., 1963), p. 27.

A new lamp   *James E. Talmage*

*O*ne summer evening as I sat musing studiously and rest-
fully in the open air outside the door of the room where I
lodged and studied, a stranger approached. I noticed that he
carried a satchel. He was affable and entertaining. I brought
another chair from within, and we chatted together till the
twilight had deepened into darkness.

Then he said, "You're a student, and doubtless have
much work to do at night. What kind of lamp do you use?"
And without waiting for a reply he continued, "I have a superior kind of lamp I should like to show you—a lamp
designed and constructed according to the latest achieve-
ments of science, far surpassing anything heretofore produced in artificial lighting."

I replied with confidence, "My friend, I have a lamp,
one that has been tested and proved. It has been a companion and friend through many a long night. I have
trimmed and cleaned it today; it is ready for lighting."

We entered my room, and I put a match to my well-
trimmed lamp. My visitor was high in his praise. It was the
best lamp of its kind, he said, and he had never seen a lamp
in better trim. He turned the wick up and down and
pronounced the judgment perfect. "Now," he said, "with
your permission I'll light my lamp." He took it from his
satchel. It had a chimney which, compared with mine, was a
factory smokestack alongside a house flue. Its hollow wick
was wide enough to admit my four fingers. Its light made a
glow to bring out the remotest corner of my room. Its
brilliant blaze made the flame in my lamp weak and pale.
Until that time of convincing demonstration, I had never
known the dim obscurity that I had lived, labored, studied,
and struggled under. "I'll buy your lamp," I said. "You need
not explain or argue further." That same night I took the
lamp to the laboratory and found that it burned with fully
four times the intensity of my student lamp.

Two days later I met the lamp peddler on the street

about noon. He answered my question that business was good. But I asked, "You are not working today?"

His rejoinder was a lesson. "Do you think I would be foolish as to go around trying to sell lamps in the daytime? Would you have bought one if I had lighted it for you when the sun was shining? I chose the time to show the superiority of my lamp over yours, and you were eager to buy a better one."

Such is the story. Now consider the application of a very small part thereof.

"Let your light so shine before men, that they may see your good works, and glorify your Father which is in heaven." (Matthew 5:16.)

The man who would sell a lamp did not disparage mine. He placed his greater light alongside my feebler flame, and I hastened to obtain it. The missionary servants of the church of Jesus Christ today are sent forth, not to assail nor to ridicule the beliefs of men, but to set before the world a superior light by which the smoky dimness of the flickering flames of man-made creeds shall be apparent. The work of the church is constructive not destructive.

Improvement Era, January 1914, pp. 256-58.

Planting
the seed
Orin R. Woodbury

*I*n 1960 it was my privilege to take my wife, brother, and sister-in-law on a personally conducted tour of Hawaii, where I had served as a missionary some twenty years before. Since this was my first trip back since my mission experience, I desired to visit the areas where I had been assigned to labor. Preparations for the journey included a careful reading of my missionary journal, to sharpen my memory of names, places, and events.

We decided to attend church our first Sunday at Kaimuki Ward, which included the area where I had first been assigned as a missionary. At priesthood meeting the high priests group was taught by a very knowledgeable and effective Chinese instructor. In response to my inquiry after meeting, I learned that he was a pharmacist by profession and that he and his wife were set-apart temple workers. His name was Kwai Shoon Lung, and he had only been a member of the Church for approximately fifteen years.

During the interval between priesthood meeting and Sunday School, we took the opportunity of becoming acquainted with others who were also waiting for the next meeting. Upon hearing my name, an impressive young man (in his early thirties) exclaimed, "Are you Elder Woodbury who was a missionary here in about 1940 or '41?"

To my affirmative answer, he expressed great joy in having "found" me. "You and your companion were the first to bring the gospel to our home," he said. His name was Glenn Lung and he explained that he lived in the family home on Ninth Avenue. His home was indeed in the area in which we had labored, so it seemed quite possible that we might have contacted him, but the name didn't seem familiar to me.

It had been my good fortune as a new missionary to have been assigned to an outstanding senior companion, Elder Ralph G. Chalker, who had maintained a full schedule of cottage meetings throughout each day and evening. We had used the "Fulness of Times" records in our presentation. Because of the numerous meetings we held, I had recorded in my journal only those involving a special faith-promoting incident or reflections regarding a person or family who seemed to be the most likely candidates for baptism. Unfortunately, I had recorded little in the early days of my mission, and I felt certain that Glenn Lung's name did not appear in my journal.

When I expressed no recognition or remembrance of his name, he explained, "Oh, you wouldn't remember me. I was only a twelve-year-old boy then, but perhaps you might remember my sister, Lydia. She was in a body cast from her neck to her knees."

This indeed rang a bell! I remember our calling at their home and asking to be allowed to share with them our message, which included a recording of an interesting historical story. Hesitant at first, the lady of the house said that we could come in on condition that we would play our record in the bedroom where her daughter, who lay in a body cast, might hear it.

"Yes," Glenn said, "that was my mother—and I was the twelve-year-old boy who sat at the end of the bed."

We had returned to their home three more times, but on our next visit, the mother had advised us that her daughter was not there, and she therefore no longer needed to be entertained. In my immature mind I had written them off as *"hoopaumanawa"* (a waste of time). Shortly thereafter, I was transferred to another island.

Glenn said that something had been said in one of those meetings that made an impression on him. "You declared that baptism was the key to the gateway of heaven," he said, "and I could not forget it." About a year later he expressed his feelings to his mother that if baptism were such an important key, they should know more about it. She agreed, and they contacted the elders, were taught the gospel, and were baptized a few months later. Some four years later, his father (the high priests group leader) and most of Glenn's brothers and sisters joined the Church. He reviewed some of the family accomplishments in church service since then, including the great number of endowments and sealings his parents had performed in the temple, and told of their uniquely successful efforts in Chinese genealogy. Then he added modestly, "and I have been found worthy to serve as a counselor in the bishopric."

He said they had been able to communicate with and express their appreciation to the elders who had baptized and confirmed them, but now they were so happy to be able to thank us for planting the seed of the gospel in their home.

Glenn's parents invited us to spend an evening in their home, where we met and visited with the entire Lung family and were privileged to hear of their experiences and to see the magnificent genealogy charts Brother Kwai Shoon Lung had prepared in both English and Chinese characters. This led to a reciprocal visit to our home in Utah and continuing relationship by correspondence. Approximately two years after our first visit, Glenn's mother, Sister Gladys Lung, informed us that her son, Glenn Y.M. Lung, had been ordained a bishop (the first Chinese bishop in the Church).

Bishop Lung's parents were subsequently called to serve as genealogical missionaries in Hong Kong, where, in addition to their genealogical research, their excellent knowledge of the Chinese language and their testimonies of the gospel afforded them many opportunities to assist the proselyting missionaries in testifying of the truth of the gospel in the investigators' native language.

Another important event occurred while we were serving as missionaries in Hawaii a few years later.* We were privileged to attend a stake conference of Honolulu Stake where Glenn Y.M. Lung was sustained as stake president.

He is still serving in this capacity at this writing. One can only speculate on how many lives have been affected for good as a result of the noble dedication of this family. Likewise, one can only wonder how many other "Lung families" have blossomed, without the realization ever com-

---

*Brother Woodbury served as president of the mission, 1966-69.

ing to the specific missionaries who, in the course of their day-to-day obedient and sometimes discouraging labors, planted the seed that would grow into a productive fruitful bough in the Lord's vineyard.

Index